ORACLE
PROTECT YOUR DATA

ORACLE
PROTECT YOUR DATA

Floribert TCHOKO

authorHOUSE®

AuthorHouse™
1663 Liberty Drive
Bloomington, IN 47403
www.authorhouse.com
Phone: 1-800-839-8640

Published by AuthorHouse   04/25/2012

ISBN: 978-1-4678-9620-7 (sc)
ISBN: 978-1-4678-9621-4 (e)

In memory of my parents
DJAPE Henri-Ledoux and **TIONGOUE Clotilde**.

FORWARD

For who is this book?

This book is for all those wishing to protect their data stored in the RDBMS ORACLE. It assumes that the reader already knows the architecture of the Oracle database (9i Versions at minimum)

Book contents

The book comprises 11 chapters divided into two parts:

I. -The first part dealing with the backup consists of four chapters

The first chapter is devoted to the logical backup
The second chapter deals with the physical backup
The third chapter discusses the various flashback technologies
The fourth chapter describes the duplication of a database
and Tablespace Point in Time Recovery

II. -The second part dealing with DATA GUARD consists of seven chapters

Begins with an overview of Data Guard in Chapter 5.
It continues with chapters 6 and 7 which respectively describe how to create a physical standby database and a logical standby database.
Chapter 8 discusses the data protection methods and redo log transfer services.
Chapter 9 describes the permutations of roles and base change.
Chapter 10 describes Fast Start Failover & Transparent Application Fail Over functionalities.
Chapter 11, which closes the last part of the book, presents other accounts related to Data Guard.

Form of the book

The book is designed as a course. It outlines in a phased manner different fundamentals of Backup / Recovery and protection against disasters. The pedagogical approach used in this book will satisfy both the needs of:

1) Beginners readers with a minimal experience in running an Oracle database who will be guided throughout this book from a database creation to Data Guard implementation through the different backups / recoveries setups procedures.

2) Students, Engineers, Project Managers who already have a first experience in administering Oracle databases and want to broaden the concepts in order to :
   - Implementing advanced backup strategies
   - Effectively protecting their data against all types of failures.

Many examples present in this book and the scripts downloadable on the site www.tchoko-books.com will enable readers to implement effective strategies for Backup /Recovery and DATA GUARD management.

The content is based on 11g version while highlighting the changes from the earlier versions 10g and 9i.

Errata and Additional Material

Despite our best endeavors, there may be errors and omissions throughout this book. While we apologize in advance for these, we will maintain up-to-date errata on the web site http://www.tchoko-books. com which will also contain additional material. You can also contact the author using the E-mail address tchokoflo@yahoo.fr.

SYMBOLS and CONVENTIONS USED

$\in$	: Belongs to
$\notin$	: Does not belong to
$>$	: Great than
$<$	: Less than
$>=$	: Great or Equal
$<=$	: Less or Equal
$< >$	: Different
{ }	:Set
[ ]	:Interval
Σ	:Sum
I/O	: Input/output
DDL	: Data Definition Language
DML	: Data Manipulation Language
OS	: Operating System

For SQL/SQL+/RMAN Commands, the following conventions are used:

[Element]   : Element between brackets is optional

{Element}   : Element underlined is the default value in a list

{elt1 | elt2 | eltn}   : A required element on choice

[elt1 | elt2 | eltn]   : An optional element on choice

Contents

PART I   BACKUPS

PART II   DATA GUARD

Floribert TCHOKONGOUE

Telecom Paris Engineer and Oracle Certified Master, Floribert TCHOKONGOUE is a senior consultant technology at Catalyst Business Solutions, Oracle platinum partner. He has 27 years experience in the IT industry with 15 years in Oracle Server technologies. During all these years, he teaches the basic database trainings as well as advanced database trainings in Oracle University classes covering:

- Real Application Clusters (RAC)
- Performance & Tuning
- Advanced Backups
- Application Server
- Grid Control
- Database Security
- Data Guard, Oracle Streams, ...

Building on his long experience of administering databases (from version 7 to 11g), and trainings delivered, he designed this book as a course. Each concept developed begins with a theoretical description followed by examples and workshops where frequent encountered errors are highlighted.

ACKNOWLEDGMENTS

I would like to thank CATALYST management (especially Prosanta Kumar Rey, Amol Awasthi and Anupam Awasthi) who encouraged me to write the English version of this book, my first production being only in French language.

I would also like to thank my wife Eliane for her coordination of the works of redaction and for her patience and support over the past 12 months, the same for my children Andress, Florient, Cindy and Leon-Marie.

Floribert TCHOKO

PRESENTATION OF DATA PROTECTION

PRESENTATION OF DATA PROTECTION

A key responsibility of the database administrator (DBA) is to ensure the availability of the database. For this, he may take the following measures in order to reduce downtime of the database:

- Multiplex control files;
- Create Redo log files groups with several members;
- Distribution of control files and files members Redo logfiles on several different disks.

Despite these precautions, an incident may still occur interrupting production. The DBA must then restore the continuity of the service as soon as possible with minimal loss of data.

Types of incidents

The incidents that may occur have various causes:

- User error;
- Instance failure;
- Block corruption;
- Physical failure

  ➢ **User error**
  A user may intentionally (or not):

  - delete a table or a tablespace;
  - truncate a table;
  - validate errors in a table.

To limit this type of error, the DBA must train users to manipulate the database and grant them only the required privileges for their work.

➤ **Block Corruption**

There are 2 types of corruptions:

- physical corruption
- logical corruption

A logical corruption corresponds to an oracle internal error. Once an inconsistency in the structure of a block is detected, it is marked as damaged. This block can in some cases be read by low-level tools. On the other side in case of a physical corruption, the block has an incorrect format. Even with a low level tool, this block can't be read. The corruptions are generally due to faulty hardware (disks, disk controllers) or problems of operating systems. To limit this type of errors, the DBA to its level,—in addition to the choice of hard disks, disk controllers, power quality and redundancy implementation thereof—made by the system administrator can prevent corruption by assigning appropriate values to certain initialization parameters. In addition, it is not recommended to run check disk utility on Oracle drives.

➤ **Instance failures**

An instance failure can occur for one of the following reasons:

- The server becomes unavailable due to a power failure or a failure of one of its hardware components other than the hard disk (CPU, RAM . . .)
- Failure of the operating system
- Failure in a background process of the Oracle server.

This type of incident does not require any action of recovery (from the backups from the DBA). He should only after resolution of the incident restart the instance and open the database. The recovery process is made by the SMON process.

➤ **Physical failures**

The physical failure, defined here as the inability to access a file needed to run the database, is the most severe type of incident, since it usually requires the intervention of the DBA that depending on the nature of the failure, may go to the full restoration of the database backup.

BACKUP/RESTORE STRATEGIES

The backup strategies vary according to operational requirements of each organism. An organization chart operating 24 hours out of 24, 7 days on 7, 365 days per year and an outage of a few minutes would result in a considerable financial loss, will not apply the same strategy that an organization chart operating five days on 7, 8 hours per day and capable of supporting shortages of more than one hour.

In the first case, one has to resort to an ONLINE backup, database open, whereas in the latter case, one might settle for a closed base backup (the data created between backups being lost and to be re-entered manually). In all cases, the strategies put in place depend on the QoS (quality of service), whose main parameters are:

- MTTR (Mean Time To Repair), expresses the time of restart of the database after incident
- MTBF (Mean time Between Failure)

In the first case of our example of continuous operation (MTTR close to 0 and MTBF near infinity), the DBA should:

- Perform ONLINE backups;
- Distribute the files in the database on mirror disks or RAID systems if possible;
- Enable the prevention of physical and logical block corruption (see below);
- Minimize instance time recovery ;
- Have a database backup on a remote site (see the 2nd part of this book).

While in the second case, the DBA could settle for a backup, database closed at the end of each operation knowing that he runs the risk of losing data from a day of use.

BACKUPS CLASSIFICATION

Backups can be classified into two types:

- Logical backups
- Physical backups

Logical backup

Logical backup is performed by a utility (OS level) EXPORT (or Data Pump since version 10g). This utility extracts the contents of the specified tables and dependent objects and stores them in a dump file whose format is independent of the operating system.
There are 5 modes of EXPORT:

- Table;
- User;
- Tablespace;
- Transport tablespace;
- Full;

These modes will be explained in detail further in this book.

 Caution:

The objects belonging to SYS schema are never copied no matter the EXPORT mode.
SYS being the owner of the database dictionary and containing essential tables necessary for the functioning of the database, a copy of these objects, then its IMPORT into another database could compromise its integrity.

It is not recommended to use EXPORT as the only type of backup for the following reasons:

- EXPORT can 't copy contents of offline tablespaces even in full mode;

- The image of the database may no longer be the same after IMPORT, if there has been an incident requiring the recreation of the database after applying patches on the Oracle server, the objects owned by SYS are not exported
- EXPORT and IMPORT can only be used as database open. In case of loss or damage of a vital file for the database (control, system, current log or undo) the database can't be opened, our EXPORT dump file can only be used after recreating the database.

In general, we use EXPORT in addition to the backup in the case of specific operations such as:

- Moving objects from one database to another for testing purposes
- Transport of tablespace
- Reorganization of the space in the tables (method commonly used in versions prior to 10g)

Physical backup

The physical backup consists in copying the files from the database. There are 2 types of physical backups:

- backups managed by the user
- backups managed by RMAN

We use a command of the operating system (cp, Copy . . .) to copy the files from the database within the backup managed by the user. RMAN (Recovery Manager) is an Oracle utility to save and recover files from the database.

TERMINONOLOGIES USED IN BACKUPS

Full backup / Incremental backup

The full backup consists of backing up all blocks of all specified source files of the database (modified or not). The incremental backup copies only the modified blocks since the previous backup. Two levels (0 and 1) of incremental backups are supported since Oracle Database version 10g; in 9i versions, we can have more than 2. A level 0 corresponds to a full backup. A level different from 0 can be either differential or cumulative. An incremental differential backup of level N backs up all changes made since last incremental differential backup of level N or less than N. While an incremental cumulative backup of level N backs up all changes made since last incremental cumulative backup of level N-1 or less than N-1. In 10g and 11g Versions, if you specify a level greater than 1, an error won't be generated but the incremental backup will be done using level 1.

Whole database backup / Partial database backup

The whole database backup copies the entire database. During a partial backup, only a portion of the database (some data files) is copied.

Online backup / Offline backup

The online backup (also called hot backup) is performed without stopping the instance, the database remains open and operations continue to be conducted. It is said that the backup is inconsistent because data files and control files are not synchronized with the redo log files. This restored backup will require recovery before the database can be opened.

The offline backup (or cold backup) is a consistent backup because it is done after shutdown of the instance (by another method than Abort). Thus the CHECKPOINT process has been done, synchronizing all the files in the database (data, control and redo log).

Structures of the database and some initialization parameters related to Backup/Recovery/Block Corruption

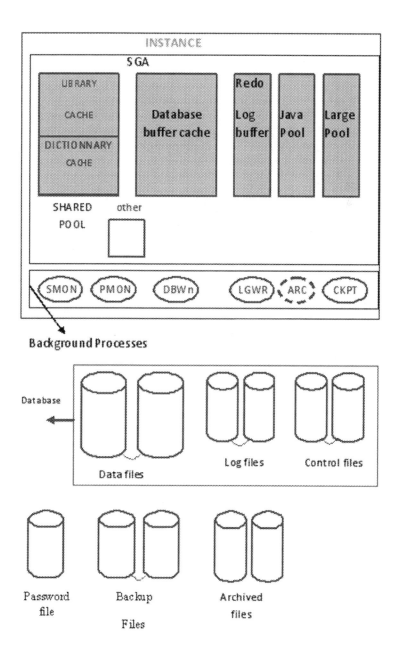

> ➢ **LARGE POOL Memory area**

Large Pool area allows allocation of I / O buffers from the SGA. It is used for:
- Backup | Restoration operations
- The I / O server processes
- Store the UGA (user Global Area) in Oracle Shared Server configuration.
- Parallel Query

> ➢ **Some initialization parameters**

DBWR_IO_SLAVES:
Indicates the number of I/O processes slaves used by the process DBWn. This parameter is used to simulate asynchronous I / O on platforms that do not support it. But even when the platform uses the asynchronous I / O we can always assign a value different from 0 to DBWR_IO_SLAVES

BACKUP_TAPE_IO_SLAVES:
Specifies whether or not the slaves I/O process are used by RMAN to back up or restore data on tape.

DB_WRITER_PROCESSES:
The number of DBWn processes, by default is 1. Specify a value different from 1 (of 2-20 in 9i/10g and up to 36 in 11gR2) if the frequency of updates of data is very IMPORTANT. Only useful if the server database has more than one CPU.
This parameter can't be defined simultaneously with DBWR_IO_SLAVES. An error will not be generated but only a single process DB_WRITER will be used.

FAST_START_MTTR_TARGET:
Recovery instance estimated time in seconds (Available since the Version 9i) is recommended instead of parameters FAST_START_IO_TARGET (which is now obsolete) and LOG_CHECKPOINT_INTERVAL.

LOG_CHECKPOINT_INTERVAL:
Number of blocks (operating system) logging that can exist between an incremental checkpoint and the last block written to the Redo Log file. Overrides the setting FAST_START_MTTR_TARGET.

LOG_CHECKPOINT_TIMEOUT:

Time in seconds elapsed since the incremental checkpoint at the last entry in the Redo Log file. Overrides the setting FAST_START_MTTR_TARGET

LOG_ARCHIVE_DEST_n:

Multiple destinations for the archived files. In Version 10g $n \in [1, 10]$ and up to 31 in 11gR2 versions

DB_BLOCK_CHECKING:

To prevent logical corruption of blocks; specifies whether a block checking is performed
(OFF | LOW | MEDIUM | HIGH)

OFF (default value):
Only blocks of the tablespace SYSTEM are subject to verification.

LOW:
The data blocks headers are checked after any change in memory (Update or Insert order)

MEDIUM:
Checks at level Low are extended to checks of blocks of tables that are not index-organized (IOT)

HIGH:
Checks at level Medium are extended to checks of blocks of IOT tables

DB_BLOCK_CHECKSUM:

Determines if a checksum is calculated and added to the header block before writing on disk
(OFF | TYPICAL | FULL)

A checksum is a number calculated from all the bytes stored in the block. At the next reading of the block, the checksum is recalculated and the stored value is checked against the calculated value. If different, the block is presumed corrupted and the operation is interrupted.

OFF:
The check applies only to SYSTEM tablespace

TYPICAL:
The checksum is calculated during operations of Reading

FULL:
The checksum is extended to the operations Update / Delete

DB_ULTRA_SAFE:
(In 11g only) used in place of the last two parameters
Values (OFF | DATA_ONLY | DATA_AND_INDEX)

DATA ONLY : equivalent to
DB_BLOCK_CHECKING = MEDIUM AND DB_BLOCK_CHECKSUM = FULL

DATA_AND_INDEX: Equivalent to:
DB_BLOCK_CHECKSUM= FULL and DB_BLOCK_CHECKING =HIGH

OFF:
The values assigned to DB_BLOCK_CHECKING AND DB_BLOCK_CHECKSUM take effect.

A Full/High value assigned to these two parameters can cause an overload of your system up to 10%. First privilege a checking at the hard level.

FIRST PART
BACKUP

## CHAPTER 1

LOGICAL BACKUP (BY DATA PUMP)

As we saw in the presentation, EXPORT is a utility permits us to copy objects from the database into a dump file. It works by reading some of the views created during the execution of the script **CATALOG. SQL** (which calls **catexp.sql** that creates the dictionary views for EXPORT). Since version 10g, Oracle offers a new tool DATA PUMP for high speed movement of data and metadata. It may well be executed in command line (by expdp, impdp) than the web interface of Enterprise Manager. DATA PUMP can also be called via **DBMS_DATAPUMP** package.

Benefits of Data PUMP

- Ability to suspend the EXPORT/IMPORT process and restart it
- Selection of fine objects

In earlier versions, you could use the clause Query to select certain rows of tables, provided that the column on which the filter will be applied is contained in all tables to EXPORT. Now you can make a finer selection using parameters like EXCLUDE, INCLUDE and CONTENT.

- Parallel Execution
  Thanks to the PARALLEL parameter, EXPORT or IMPORT can be done in parallel
- EXPORT of a percentage of the selected objects by using the parameter SAMPLE;
- Estimaion of the space consumed by dump files by using the parameter ESTIMATE _ONLY;
- EXPORT / IMPORT in network mode;
- EXPORT or IMPORT of one database to another using parameter NETWORK_LINK;

- Explicit specification of the version of the database by using the VERSION parameter.
- Data compression during EXPORT;
- Encryption during EXPORT and decryption during IMPORT by using parameters ENCRYPTION | ENCRYPTION_PASSWORD | ENCRYPTION_ MODE | ENCRYPTION_ALGORITHM.
  (Requires a master key stored in a wallet)

Functioning of Data PUMP.

At the start of the work of Data pump, a master table is created in the database where this work is done. At the end of the job, this table is automatically deleted. The following 3 types of files are generated:

- Dump file
- Log file
- SQL file (for the creation of metadata and / or index), if the parameter SQLFILE is used when importing, this script is not automatically executed.

Unlike EXPORT / IMPORT utilities versions prior to Oracle 10g, Data pump has a feature based solely on the server side of the database rather than the client side. Thus, the parameter specifying the dump file (DUMPFILE), log and SQL files does not allow absolute file. These files are located in a directory whose order of priority is as follows:

- Directory per file, directory objects can be specified for each file (eg DUMPFILE = mydir: file. dmp)
- DIRECTORY parameter
- Environment Variable DATA_PUMP_DIR
- Directory object DATA_PUMP_DIR

The directory object is an object created by the command:

☞ SQL> CREATE DIRECTORY mydir AS '/path/';

The path should be created manually by an order in the operating system

The directory objects belong to the SYS schema, rather than the person creating it, and to be able to create, the user must have the system privilege CREATE ANY DIRECTORY. The permissions to read (for IMPORT) and write (for EXPORT) must then be granted on this directory

☞ SQL> GRANT READ, WRITE ON DIRECTORY mydir TO user1;

Data pump can use a set of dump files. The parameter DUMPFILE determines the list of files specified in two ways :

- Listing of files separated by a comma
- Using % U model, in this case, the file names are generated automatically by adding the suffix 01.02 ... ... .99

The initial number of dump files depends on the parameters PARALLEL and DUMPFILE, the FILESIZE parameter limiting the maximum size of each dump file (during EXPORT)

▶ **Caution:**

On EXPORT, the existing files are not overwritten unlike versions prior to 10g, an error is returned if it is the case unless you specify the REUSE_DUMPFILES parameter with the value Y (possible in 11g version only).

DIFFERENT METHODS OF EXPORT

EXPORT utility has five (5) modes of EXPORT:

- Table
- User
- Tablespace
- Transport Tablespace
- Database

➤ **Table mode**

This mode allows you to EXPORT:

- The metadata tables and data
- The constraints associated to tables
- The permissions granted on tables
- Indexes and triggers associated with tables (if the permissions of the user running EXPORT permits it).

➤ **User mode**

In this mode, the user can export:

- All objects belonging to him (tables, indexes, views, triggers . . .) except the indexes and triggers belonging to him but which refers to tables belonging to other users.
- Triggers and indexes created by other users on the tables owned by the user (this requires privileges).

➤ **Tablespace and Transport tablespace modes**

Since version 8i, tablespaces can be transported from one database to another (this is called transportable tablespace).

Since version 9i, you can EXPORT a tablespace.
This mode requires that the user performing the EXPORT has EXP_FULL_DATABASE or Datapump_ EXP_FULL_ DATABASE role.

Transporting tablespaces is faster as EXPORT only copies the metadata of the tablespace.

➤ **Database mode**

This mode allows you to EXPORT all objects in the database except those belonging to the schema SYS. It requires the role EXP_FULL_DATABASE

IMPORT

IMPORT reads the dump files created by the EXPORT and writes them in the database. It has five modes similar to EXPORT mode (table, user, tablespace, transport tablespace, full database).

> ## ➢ Path followed by the IMPORT of tables

1) The table is created in the tablespace where it was found at EXPORT if it exists and if the user owns the quota required. If not the IMPORT creates the table in default tablespace of the user. If creation is impossible, an error is generated and the IMPORT passes to the following table;
2) The data is loaded into the table.
3) B-TREE indexes are created
4) The index set of constraints, triggers and indexes BITMAP are created
5) The process resumes at step 1.

This order prevents data being rejected because of the order in which tables are imported. However some procedures can be terminated on the IMPORT because they are imported before the objects to which they relate.

▶ Caution:

- EXPORT and IMPORT are not necessarily symmetric that is to say, we can make such an EXPORT FULL and an IMPORT TABLE.
- IMPORT loads or attempts to load the data without clearing the tables, the DBA must first clear the existing tables before beginning the IMPORT.
- IMPORT FULL attempts by default to create tablespaces at their image during EXPORT (location and names of data files). If the creation of tablespaces is impossible the rule seen earlier will be applied to the creation of tables. If we want a database after the IMPORT

full with the image of the database prior to EXPORT, tablespaces must be created within the new database before IMPORT.

- The EXPORT or transport of tablespace does not EXPORT the types defined by the user.
- While importing tablespace, schemas are not created.

SOME EXAMPLES OF DATA PUMP USAGE

[Oracle @ camsrv3 ~] $ expdp system / oracle dumpfile = tblsp_
example.dmp logfile = export_example.log job_name = export_tblsp_
user tablespaces = example [Oracle @ camsrv3 ~] $ expdp system /
oracle attach = export_tblsp_user

EXPORT: Release 11.1.0.6.0—Production on Sunday, January 31,
2010 4:24:37 p.m.
Copyright (c) 2003, 2007, Oracle. All rights reserved.

Connected to: Oracle Database 11g Enterprise Edition Release
11.1.0.6.0—Production With the Partitioning, OLAP, Data Mining and
Real Application Testing options

Job: EXPORT_TBLSP_USER
Owner: SYSTEM
Operation: EXPORT
Private Creator: TRUE
GUID: 7E794C042E292A48E040007F01004F90
Start Time: Sunday, January 31, 2010 4:24:04 p.m.
Fashion: TABLESPACE
Instance: orcl
Max Parallelism: 1
EXPORT Job Parameters:
Parameter Name Parameter Value:
CLIENT_COMMAND system /******** tblsp_example.dmp
dumpfile = logfile = ex port_example.log job_name = export_tblsp_
user tablespaces = example
State: EXECUTING
Bytes Processed: 0
Current Parallelism: 1
Job Error Count: 0
Dump File: / u01/app/oracle/admin/orcl/dpdump/tblsp_example.dmp
bytes written: 4.096
Worker 1 Status:

Process Name: **DW01**

State: EXECUTING
Object Type:
TABLE_EXPORT / TABLE / STATISTICS / TABLE_STATISTICS
    Completed Objects: 50
    Worker Parallelism: 1

EXPORT> stop_job
Are you sure you wish to stop this job ([yes] / no): yes

[Oracle @ camsrv3 ~] $ BACK TO THE WINDOW or EXPORT is
subject cde

Processing object type TABLE_EXPORT / TABLE / STATISTICS /
TABLE_STATISTICS
Processing object type TABLE_EXPORT / TABLE / INDEX /
DOMAIN_INDEX / INDEX
Processing object type TABLE_EXPORT / TABLE / POST_
INSTANCE / PROCACT_INSTANCE
Processing object type TABLE_EXPORT / TABLE / POST_
INSTANCE / PROCDEPOBJ.. exported "HR". "INVOICE" 220.8
MB 727069 rows Job "SYSTEM". "EXPORT_TBLSP_USER"
stopped by user request at 4:25:05 p.m.

a)   **Connection to existing work by using the ATTACH parameter**
     $expdp system /oracle ATTACH = nom_Job_export

You can issue the following orders:

ADD_FILE: add a file EXPORT
ADD_FILE = [object-directory:] filename [.....]
CONTINUOUS _CLIENT: Pass from interactive mode to display
mode continuously on screen
EXIT_CLIENT: terminates the continuous display of the progress of
work without interrupting data pump
FILESIZE: redefines the size of dump files, filesize = number
HELP: displays help
KILL _JOB: stops the data pump work
START_JOB: Restarts interrupted work

STOP_JOB: suspends work
PARALLEL: Changes the degree of parallelism data pump
Parallel = number
STATUS: Specifies the display frequency of progression of work in seconds
> STATUS = seconds.

If a value is not specified, the number 0 is the default and refreshing the screen display will no longer be made.

b) Transport tablespace

$ expdp system/oracle DUMPFILE = tblsp_example.dmp TRANSPORT_TABLESPACES = example TRANSPORT_FULL_CHECK = {Y|N}

The parameter TRANSPORT_FULL_CHECK applicable only in transport tablespace mode specifies whether the verification of dependencies between objects of tablespaces to transport and these out of these tablespaces must be checked, default value to N.

Y: checking dependency is done in two senses. For example, if the table is in the set to transport and the index is out of this set an error is reported and the Export stops. Similarly, if the index appears in the set to be transported and the the table table out of this set, Export ends with error.

N: The check is only conducted to determine whether dependent objects are in the set (an index depends on a table but not vice versa), so if the table is in the set but not the index there is no error. By cons, if the index is in the set but not the table, there is an error because an index without table has no meaning.

Before starting, you can check the 'self-contained' of the tablespace by running:

```
SQL>exec sys.dbms_tts.transport_set_check( 'tblsp',
TRUE,TRUE|FALSE );
```

```
SQL>select * from sys.transport_set_violations;
To get the list of objects violating the 'self content'
```

The third parameter corresponds to the parameter TRANSPORT_FULL_CHECK of the expdp command.

▶ **Caution:**

- Note that in tablespace mode EXPORT (not transport tablespace), the indexes are still exported even if they are outside the tablespace that you want to EXPORT.
- Tablespaces to be moved must first be in READ ONLY mode.
- The source and destination databases must use the same character set

When Export is completed, data files associated with tablespaces to transport and dump generated are copied to the target system (via ftp, cp or any other utility), then the IMPORT command is executed on the target
$ impdp system /oracle TRANSPORT_DATAFILES = / path / file
DUMPFILE = tbsp_example.dmp.
In the parameter TRANSPORT_DATAFILES, you specify the data files copied earlier.

▶ **note**

- Do not specify the parameter TRANSPORT_TABLESPACES when importing only if the latter is done in the network mode (e.g. specifying the parameter NETWORK_LINK)
- Schemas to witch belong the objects in the tablespaces to be imported must exist in the target database before starting the IMPORT, otherwise an error is generated and those objects and skipped.
- The types defined by the user must be created manually.
- Reset the tablespaces in Read-write mode after the import.

c) Filtering during Data Pump.

- Select the type of objects with the parameters INCLUDE | EXCLUDE {(INCLUDE | EXCLUDE) = (type _objet [: expression]}

- Select data with the parameters CONTENT and QUERY CONTENT = (ALL | METADATA_ONLY | DATA_ONLY) QUERY = [schema.] [Table Name:] = "query clause"

Example

```
$ expdp system/oracle dumpfile = export_schemas.dmp
Shemas=sh,hr
EXCLUDE = VIEW
EXCLUDE = PROCEDURE: 'LIKE secure%'
CONTENT = ALL
QUERY = hr.employees: ''Where salary <10000''
```

EXPORT of objects of users sh, hr excluding views, procedures beginning with secure and employees whose salary is above 10,000. The exclusion of an object also causes the exclusion of dependent objects (eg excluding a table will result in exclusion of associated indexes and triggers). It is the same for IMPORT.
EXCLUDE and INCLUDE are mutually exclusive.

EXAMPLE USING ENTERPRISE MANAGER

☞ caution: Data Pump cannot be used with the user Sys

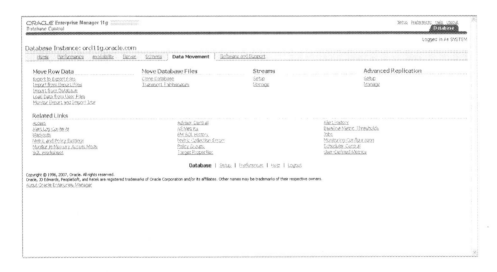

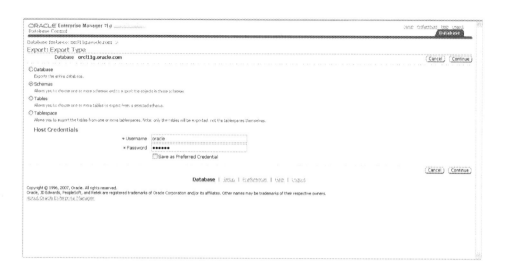

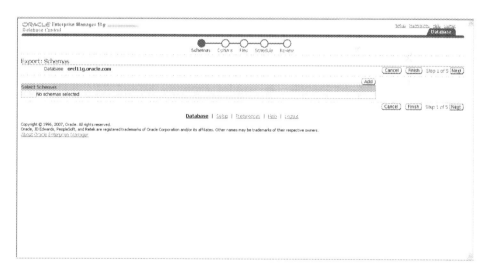

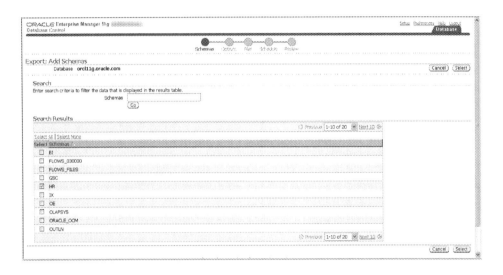

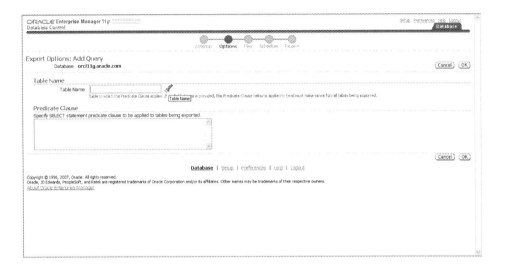

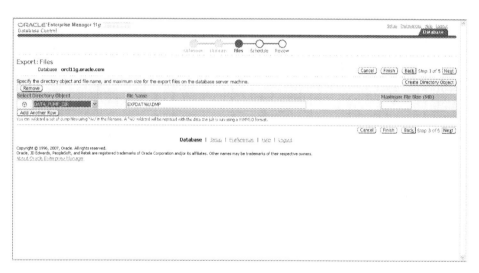

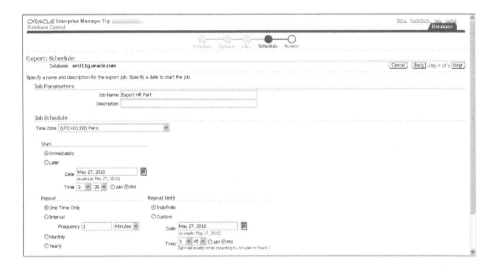

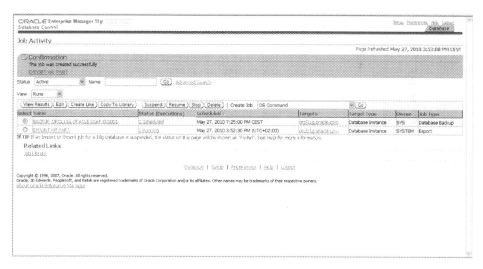

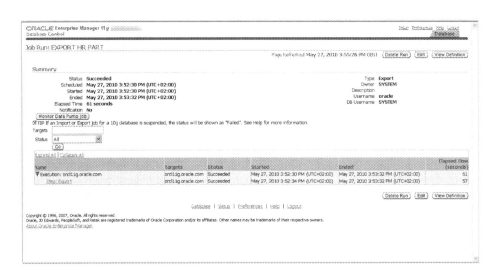

ORACLE Enterprise Manager 11g
Database Control

Setup Preferences Help Logout
Database

Job Run: EXPORT HR PART 2

Step: Export

Page Refreshed May 27, 2010 3:55:35 PM CEST

View Data Manual Refresh

Status **Succeeded**	Started **May 27, 2010 3:52:34 PM (UTC+02:00)**
Exit Code **0**	Ended **May 27, 2010 3:53:32 PM (UTC+02:00)**
Step ID **23591**	Step Elapsed Time **58 seconds**
Targets **orcl11g.oracle.com**	Management Service **server1.oracle.com:1158_Management_Service**
	☑ TIP Management Service from which the job step was dispatched.

Output Log

```
Job EXPORT HR PART has been reopened at Thursday, 27 May, 2010 15:52
Restarting "SYSTEM"."EXPORT HR PART":
Estimate in progress using BLOCKS method...
Processing object type SCHEMA_EXPORT/TABLE/TABLE_DATA
.  estimated "HR"."COUNTRIES"                  64 KB
.  estimated "HR"."DEPARTMENTS"                 64 KB
.  estimated "HR"."EMPLOYEES"                   64 KB
.  estimated "HR"."EMP_TEST"                    64 KB
.  estimated "HR"."JOBS"                        64 KB
.  estimated "HR"."JOB_HISTORY"                 64 KB
.  estimated "HR"."LOCATIONS"                   64 KB
.  estimated "HR"."REGIONS"                     64 KB
Total estimation using BLOCKS method: 512 KB
Processing object type SCHEMA_EXPORT/USER
Processing object type SCHEMA_EXPORT/SYSTEM_GRANT
Processing object type SCHEMA_EXPORT/ROLE_GRANT
Processing object type SCHEMA_EXPORT/DEFAULT_ROLE
Processing object type SCHEMA_EXPORT/PRE_SCHEMA/PROCACT_SCHEMA
Processing object type SCHEMA_EXPORT/SEQUENCE/SEQUENCE
Processing object type SCHEMA_EXPORT/TABLE/TABLE
Processing object type SCHEMA_EXPORT/TABLE/GRANT/OWNER_GRANT/OBJECT_GRANT
Processing object type SCHEMA_EXPORT/TABLE/INDEX/INDEX
Processing object type SCHEMA_EXPORT/TABLE/CONSTRAINT/CONSTRAINT
Processing object type SCHEMA_EXPORT/TABLE/INDEX/STATISTICS/INDEX_STATISTICS
Processing object type SCHEMA_EXPORT/TABLE/COMMENT
```

## CHAPTER 2

PHYSICAL BACKUPS

There are two types of physical backups:

- Backup managed by the user
- Backup managed by RMAN (Recovery Manager)

II-1 BACKUP & RECOVERY MANAGED BY THE USER

II-1-a BACKUPS MANAGED BY THE USER

The backup managed by the user is performed using the operating system commands to copy files from the database to a backup location. It requires knowledge of the names and locations of files to be backed up. It can be carried base open or closed base. The opened database backup requires that the database is in ARCHIVELOG mode.
Follow these steps to set the database in ARCHIVELOG mode

SQL> SHUTDOWN IMMEDIATE;
SQL> STARTUP MOUNT EXCLUSIVE;
SQL> ALTER DATABASE ARCHIVELOG;
SQL> ALTER DATABASE OPEN;

▶ Caution:

In NOARCHIVELOG mode, it is also possible to save and restore a tablespace if it is offline or in read-only mode.

➤ TOTAL OFFLINE BACKUP

All data files and control files must be backed up. Even though it is not necessary to save the redo logfiles, we recommend it in this mode, because if not backed up, after restoring data files and control files, we should make an incomplete recovery before returning database available. The views V$DATAFILE (or DBA_DATA_FILES), V$LOGFILE, V$CONTROLFILE, respectively, contain information on the data files, log files and control files. Before starting the backup, you should consult these views to get the names and locations of various files to back up.

```
SELECT Name, status FROM V$DATAFILE;
SELECT Name, status FROM V$CONTROLFILE;
SELECT Member FROM V$LOGFILE;
```

☞ It is not necessary to save the temp files, as they will be recreated at the instance startup.

The file and their location located are then integrated into a script that will be launched the database closed.

(Example on Windows):

```
COPY C:\oracle\oradata\SYSTEM2\SYSTEM01.DBF C:\save_data\SYSTEM01.dbf
COPY C:\ ...... \RBS01.DBF C:\save_data \RBs01.dbf
COPY C:\oracle\oradata\DEMO\REDO01.LOG C:\save_data\REDO01.Log.
```

▶ Remark

A dynamic script can be written that take into account additions or deletions of new files in the database.

₂Dynamic script backup

Spool off
Set echo off
Set lines 200
Set pagesize 0

Set newpage 0
Set space 0
Set heading off
Set feedback off
Set term off
Spool c: \ save_db.bat
Select 'COPY' | | TRIM (NAME) | | 'C: \ save_data \' FROM
V$CONTROLFILE;
Select 'COPY' | | TRIM (MEMBER) | | 'C: \ save_data \' FROM
V$LOGFILE;
Select 'COPY' | | TRIM (NAME) | | 'C: \ save_data \' FROM
V$DATAFILE;
Spool off

Content generated spool:

COPY C: \ oracle \ oradata \ DEMO \ SYSTEM01.DBF C: \ save_data
COPY C: \ oracle \ oradata \ DEMO \ RBS01.DBF C: \ save_data
COPY C: \ oracle \ oradata \ DEMO \ USERS01.DBF C: \ save_data
COPY C: \ oracle \ oradata \ DEMO \ TEMP01.DBF C: \ save_data
COPY C: \ oracle \ oradata \ DEMO \ TOOLS01.DBF C: \ save_data
COPY C: \ oracle \ oradata \ DEMO \ INDX01.DBF C: \ save_data
COPY C: \ oracle \ oradata \ DEMO \ DR01.DBF C: \ save_data
COPY C:\oracle\oradata\DEMO\OEM_REPOSITORY.ORAC:\save_data
COPY C: \ oracle \ oradata \ DEMO \ CONTROL01.CTL C: \ save_data
COPY C: \ oracle \ oradata \ DEMO \ CONTROL02.CTL C: \ save_data
COPY C: \ oracle \ oradata \ DEMO \ CONTROL03.CTL C: \ save_data
COPY C: \ oracle \ oradata \ DEMO \ REDO01.LOG C: \ save_data
COPY C: \ oracle \ oradata \ DEMO \ REDO02.LOG C: \ save_data
COPY C: \ oracle \ oradata \ DEMO \ REDO03.LOG C: \ save_data

The offline backup has the advantage of being easy to implement and once the script written, the DBA intervention is unnecessary.

Its main inconveniences are:

-   Loss of data since the last backup in case of restoration
-   During the backup (which can be long depending on file size and system resources) the database is unavailable

ONLINE BACKUP

In organizations operating continuously, the online backup must be made in the following conditions:

- Database in ARCHIVELOG mode
- Redo logfiles archived (archiving is automatic once the database is placed in ARCHIVELOG mode since version 10g).

All files or part of the data files of a tablespace can be backed up. In both cases, the database remains available during the backup.

For the backup of a tablespace online, follow these steps:

1) Put the tablespace in backup mode with the command
   SQL> ALTER TABLESPACE tblsp_name BEGIN BACKUP;
   This freezes the sequence number in the datafile header data and allows redo logs to be applied from the beginning of the backup in case of recovery.
2) Using a Backup utility of the operating system, copy all the data files of the tablespace to the backup storage location.

▶ **Remark**

- In Windows systems, choose the command OCOPY,a copy utility command of Oracle to avoid an error message "File in use"

3) When the copies of all data files of tablespace completed, end the backup tablespace with the command
   SQL > ALTER TABLESPACE tblsp_name END BACKUP;
4) Archive the log files that are not yet using the command:
   SQL > ALTER SYSTEM ARCHIVE LOG CURRENT ;
   Repeat steps 1-4 for all tablespaces, tablespace system and undo included.

Views of the data dictionary to check

- V$BACKUP
  The STATUS column indicates whether the tablespaces whose file numbers are specified by FILE # is yes (ACTIVE) or not (NOT ACTIVE) in backup mode

- V$DATAFILE_HEADER
  The FUZZY column (YES or NO value) also indicates whether the tablespace whose numbers specified by FILE # file is in backup mode

- V$DATAFILE or DBA_DATA_FILES
  Should be consulted for a list of files associated with TABLESPACES

The view DBA_DATA_FILES contains both the names of data files and tablespace names. But this view as all non-dynamic view is not available when the database is in the state MOUNT. For this reason it is best to do a join between V$TABLESPACE and V$DATAFILE for a list of all data files per TABLESPACE.

List of tablespace data files

```
SQL> select t.ts #, t.name, substr (d.name, 1.60)
DATA_FILE
2 from v$tablespace t, v$datafile d WHERE t.ts# = d.ts#
order by t.name;
6 DRSYS C:\ORACLE\ORADATA\DEMO\DR01.DBF
5 INDX C:\ORACLE\ORADATA\DEMO\
7 OEM_REPOSITORY C:\ORACLE\ORADATA\DEMO\OEM_
REPOSITORY.ORA
1 RBS C:\ORACLE\ORADATA\DEMO\RBS01.DBF
0 SYSTEM C:\ORACLE\ORADATA\DEMO\SYSTEM01.DBF
3 TEMP C:\ORACLE\ORADATA\DEMO\TEMP01.DBF
4 TOOLS C:\ORACLE\ORADATA\DEMO\TOOLS01.DBF
2 USERS C:\ORACLE\ORADATA\DEMO\USERS01.DBF
```

Saving a tablespace in read-only mode

When a tablespace is made read-only, a checkpoint is done, then data files and control files headers are updated with the SCN (System Change Number) of the redo logfile. A normal backup (by operating system copy command or utility OCOPY) must be performed for just restore the data files in case of damage. If this backup is not made, a recovery from the archives and probably on line redo log will be necessary.

Failure during a tablespace backup

During backup of a tablespace file, database open, there may be an incident making the data file unusable.

On restarting the instance, the database will not open because the file header data has been frozen by the order.
```
SQL>ALTER TABLESPACE .... BEGIN BACKUP
```
and is no longer synchronized with the Redo Log File. To remedy this problem you must:

1) Check the V$BACKUP view to identify the data file being backed up;
2) Run the command.

```
SQL > ALTER DATABASE DATAFILE file_number END BACKUP;
                        or
SQL > ALTER DATABASE END BACKUP;
```

▶ **Caution:**

You cannot execute the command **SQL > ALTER TABLESPACE tblsp_name END BACKUP** because the database is in mount state and tablespaces are accessible only to state OPEN.

Manual controlfile backup

Given the vital importance of the control file to start the database, a manual backup of this file is recommended. If you lose all control files, the start of the instance, database even MOUNT state is impossible. You can save the file controls in one of the following ways:

1) By creating a binary image by the command
   SQL>ALTER DATABASE BACKUP CONTROLFILE TO file-name;

2) By creating a script text (executable in SQL) by the command
   SQL>ALTER DATABASE BACKUP CONTROLFILE TO TRACE;

Generates a trace file in the destination specified by USER_DUMP_DEST which name is <SID>_ora_PID.trc. This file must be renamed to have an extension sql and launch to recreate the control file

Example trace of control file

SQL> alter database backup control file to trace;
Database altered.
RESULT PRODUCT

Dump file C: \ oracle \ admin \ demo \ udump \ ORA00500.TRC
Tue Nov. 16 2004 2:05:56 p.m.
ORACLE V8.1.7.0.0—Production vsnsta = 0
Vsnsql vsnxtr = e = 3
Windows 2000 Version 5.0 Service Pack 2, CPU type 586
Oracle8i Enterprise Edition Release 8.1.7.0.0—Production
JServer Release 8.1.7.0.0—Production
Windows 2000 Version 5.0 Service Pack 2, CPU type 586
Instance name: demo
Redo thread mounted by this instance: 1
Oracle process number: 26
Windows thread id: 500, image: ORACLE.EXE
*** SESSION ID: (10.3778) 2004-11-16 14:05:56.123
*** 2004-11-16 14:05:56.123
# The commands FOLLOWING Will create a new control file and use it
# To open the database.
# Data Used by the recovery manager Will Be Lost. Additional logs May

Be # required for media recovery of offline data files. Use this
Only if the current version of all online logs are available.
STARTUP nomount
CREATE   CONTROLFILE   REUSE   DATABASE   "DEMO"
NORESETLOGS NOARCHIVELOG
MAXLOGFILES 32
MAXLOGMEMBERS 2
MAXDATAFILES 254
MaxInstance 1
MAXLOGHISTORY 1815
LOGFILE
GROUP 1 'C: \ oracle \ oradata \ DEMO \ REDO01.LOG' SIZE 1M,
GROUP 2 'C: \ oracle \ oradata \ DEMO \ REDO02.LOG' SIZE 1M,
GROUP 3 'C: \ oracle \ oradata \ DEMO \ REDO03.LOG' SIZE 1M
DATAFILE
'C: \ oracle \ oradata \ DEMO \ SYSTEM01.DBF'
'C: \ oracle \ oradata \ DEMO \ RBS01.DBF'
'C: \ oracle \ oradata \ DEMO \ USERS01.DBF'
'C: \ oracle \ oradata \ DEMO \ TEMP01.DBF'
'C: \ oracle \ oradata \ DEMO \ TOOLS01.DBF'
'C: \ oracle \ oradata \ DEMO \ INDX01.DBF'
'C: \ oracle \ oradata \ DEMO \ DR01.DBF'
'C: \ oracle \ oradata \ DEMO \ OEM_REPOSITORY.ORA'
CHARACTER SET WE8ISO8859P1;
Recovery # IS required if "any of the datafiles are restored backups,
Or if the last shutdown Was Not Normal or immediate.
RECOVER DATABASE
Database can now Be Opened Normally.
ALTER DATABASE OPEN;
No tempfile entries found to add.

Addition of a control file can be done by:

1) Shutdown the instance
2) Copy by an operating system command control files specified by
   the parameter control_files
3) Add this new file in the list of parameter control_files
4) Start the instance and open the database

The following commands (change of the configuration database) cause changes in the control file:

CREATE | DROP TABLESPACE
ALTER DATABASE {ADD | DROP} [STANDBY] LOGFILE .... }
ALTER DATABASE {ADD | DROP} LOGFILE GROUP
ALTER DATABASE {ARCHIVELOG | NOARCHIVELOG}
ALTER DATABASE RENAME FILE
ALTER TABLESPACE {READ ONLY | READ WRITE}
ALTER TABLESPACE {ADD | RENAME} DATAFILE

It is therefore recommended to backup the control file after running one of these commands

II-1-B. RECOVERY MANAGED BY THE USER

PRESENTATION

The restoration is based on the type of backup and archiving mode of the database.

In NOARCHIVELOG mode, we have seen that in general one performs a whole database backup (data file, control file, Redo logfiles) base closed. When an incident requiring a restore occurs, all files saved should be restored to their original location, base closed by a command of the operating system.
No recovery is necessary and once the restoration is complete the database is made available to users by the command **SQL > STARTUP....**

In this recovery mode, data generated after the backup are lost!

There are two types of recoveries permitting either not to lose any data or retrieve data to a specific earlier stage. These are:

- Complete recovery
- Incomplete recovery

II-1-b-1. COMPLETE RECOVERY

 Caution:

The database must be in ARCHIVELOG mode. This type of recovery is used in case of loss of one or more data files. Recovery can be made base open unless the file to recover belongs to the tablespace SYSTEM or a tablespace containing active rollback segments (Undo Tablespace). The archived log files (plus current logfiles if needed) are applied for the recovery of lost files to their condition before the incident.

Steps to follow :

1 - Observe

Before any action, it is recommended to consult the alert.log file and data dictionary views as follows:

V$RECOVER_FILE: contains file numbers, status and error of files that require recovery
V$DATAFILE: name of the data files of the database (for use with V$RECOVER_FILE)
V$BACKUP: contains the files being in hot backup. Very useful if a system failure occurred while a hot backup was in progress.
V$ARCHIVED_LOG: contains the archived log.
V$RECOVERY_LOG: contains all the archived files necessary to the recovery.
V$DATAFILE_HEADER: status of data files (ONLINE or OFFLINE)
V$LOG_HISTORY: history of logs.

2 - Restore
Restore only the data files to retrieve.

Do not restore the control files, or Redo Log files Online

3 - Ensure

The V$Recovery_Log view lists files needed for recovery. We must ensure their existence and their location in the directory specified by LOG_ARCHIVE_DEST_n

4 - Apply the RECOVER command

5 - Make the database available

▶ **Caution:**

Before you restore a damaged file, you can check the contents of the backup with utility dbv whose syntax is:

$ dbv file = file_name START = start_block \
END = end_block LOGFILE = file_log blocksize=size_block

EXAMPLES OF COMPLETE RECOVERY OF DATA

1) LOSS OF A DATA FILE (BASE INITIALLY CLOSED)

a)   At the start of the instance, the database can no longer open. The error message is reported at the opening of the database and recorded in the alert file

SQL> connect / as sysdba
Connected to an idle instance.
SQL> startup;
ORACLE instance started.
Total System Global Area 73164828 bytes
Fixed Size 75804 bytes
Variable Size 56233984 bytes
Database Buffers 16777216 bytes
Redo Buffers 77824 bytes
Database mounted.
ORA-01157: Unable to identify or lock the data file 3—see the trace file
ORA-01110: data file 3: 'C: \ oracle \ oradata \ DEMO \ USERS01. DBF'

CONTENT OF FILE ALERT
Starting up ORACLE RDBMS Version: 8.1.7.0.0.
System parameters with non-default values:
Processes = 150
shared_pool_size = 31457280
large_pool_size = 614400
java_pool_size = 20971520
control_files = C: \ oracle \ oradata \ demo \ control01.ctl,
C: \ oracle \ oradata \ demo \ control02.ctl, C: \ oracle \ oradata \ demo \ control03.ctl
db_block_buffers = 2048
DB_BLOCK_SIZE = 8192

Compatible	= 8.1.0
log_archive_start	= TRUE

log_archive_format =%% ORACLE_SID%% T% TS% S. ARC

log_buffer = 32768

log_checkpoint_interval	= 10000
log_checkpoint_timeout	= 1800

DB_File = 1024

db_file_multiblock_read_count	= 8
max_enabled_roles	= 30
remote_login_passwordfile	= EXCLUSIVE

global_names = TRUE

distributed_transactions	= 10

instance_name = demo

SERVICE_NAME	= demo

mts_dispatchers =

(PROTOCOL = TCP) (PRE	= oracle.aurora.server.SGiopServer)

open_links = 4

sort_area_size	= 65536
sort_area_retained_size	= 65536

db_name = demo

open_cursors = 300

ifile = C: \ oracle \ admin \ demo \ pfile \ init.ora

os_authent_prefix =

job_queue_processes	= 4
job_queue_interval	= 60

parallel_max_servers = 5

background_dump_dest	= C: \ oracle \ admin \ demo \ bdump

user_dump_dest = C: \ oracle \ admin \ demo \ udump

max_dump_file_size	= 10240

oracle_trace_collection_name =

PMON started "with pid	= 2
DBW0 Started with pid	= 3
LGWR started "with pid	= 4
CKPT started "with pid	= 5
SMON started "with pid	= 6
RECO started "with pid	= 7
SNP0 Started with pid	= 8
SNP1 started "with pid	= 9
SNP2 started "with pid	= 10
SNP3 started "with pid	= 11

Tue November 16 2004 5:22:19 p.m.

Starting up 1 shared server (s) . . .

Starting up 1 dispatcher (s) for network address

'(ADDRESS = (PARTIAL = YES) (PROTOCOL = TCP))' . . .

ARCH: STARTING ARCH PROCESSES

ARC0 started "with pid   = 14

ARC0: Archival started"

Tue November 16 2004 5:22:20 p.m.

ARCH: STARTING ARCH PROCESSES COMPLETE

Tue November 16 2004 5:22:20 p.m.

ALTER DATABASE MOUNT

Tue November 16 2004 5:22:27 p.m.

Successful mount of redo thread 1, with mount id 3286480530.

Tue November 16 2004 5:22:27 p.m.

Database mounted in Exclusive Mode.

Completed: ALTER DATABASE MOUNT

Tue November 16 2004 5:22:27 p.m.

ALTER DATABASE OPEN

Tue November 16 2004 5:22:27 p.m.

Errors in file C: \ oracle \ admin \ demo \ bdump \ demoDBW0. TRC:

ORA-01157: cannot Identify / lock data file 3—see DBWR trace file

ORA-01110: data file 3: 'C: \ oracle \ oradata \ DEMO \ USERS01. DBF'

ORA-27041: Unable to open file

OSD-04002: cannot open file

O / S-Error: (OS 2) The system cannot find the file specified.

ORA-1157 signalled During: ALTER DATABASE OPEN.

Consulting the view V$DATAFILE_HEADER shows that the data file 3 is not found and its status is ONLINE. To make the database available, the file must first be put OFFLINE.

SQL > ALTER DATABASE DATAFILE 3 OFFLINE;

SQL > ALTER DATABASE OPEN;

The database is available, of course, access to the data file 3 is impossible

b) We restore the lost data file

```
SQL >HOST copy C:\save_data\users01.dbf C:\oracle\
oradata\demo
```

If the original location of the file can no longer be used (eg media failed), the file must be restored elsewhere and also the Oracle server must first be informed of the new location by the command:

```
SQL > ALTER DATABASE Rename FILE
'C: \oracle\oradata\demo\users01.dbf' TO 'D:\oradata\
user01.dbf';
```

c) **We consult the view V$Recovery_Log for a list of necessary logs to the recovery**

```
SQL > SELECT * FROM V$RECOVERY_LOG;
```

d) **We apply the recover command to the file number 3**

```
SQL > RECOVER DATAFILE 3 ;
```

e) **set back online the file number 3**

```
SQL > ALTER DATABASE DATAFILE 3 ONLINE or
SQL > ALTER TABLESPACE USERS01 ONLINE;
```

2) LOSS OF A DATA FILE WITH NO BACKUP

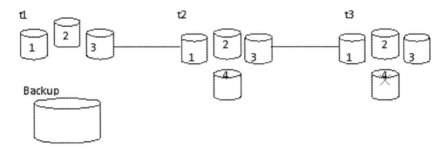

t1: Database in ARCHIVELOG mode and backup of the database made.
t2: The DBA creates a tablespace test (test_data) and creates tables inside

t3: the datafile of the tablespace test_data is damaged (disk failure), meanwhile it has never been saved.

!! The recovery of this tablespace is nevertheless possible by following the steps below:

a) Is the database available?

- If the database was opened, the loss of that file (which does not belong neither to a tablespace SYSTEM nor to a tablespace UNDO active) does not stop the database.
- If the database was closed at the time of the loss of this file, it cannot be opened at the start of the instance if it is ONLINE. We check the status in the view V$datafile_header

SQL > SELECT File, Status, ERROR FROM V$datafile_header ;

If the status of the file is ONLINE put it OFFLINE with the command:

```
SQL > ALTER DATABASE DATAFILE 11 OFFLINE
                        or
SQL > ALTER DATABASE DATAFILE 'D:\test_data.dbf' OFFLINE;
```

b) Re-create the data file by the command

ALTER DATABASE CREATE DATAFILE 'D: \test_data.dbf'
AS 'E: \test_data. dbf'

The AS clause is used to recreate the file with a new name to a new location if necessary. Here in this case the drive D: is corrupted, the file is recreated on disk E:

c) Examination of archives needed for recovery & recovery

```
SQL >SELECT * FROM V$Recovery_Log;
SQL >RECOVER Datafile 'E: \ test_data.dbf';
```

```
                           or
SQL >Recover TABLESPACE test_data ;
```

d) Setting the tablespace online

```
SQL> ALTER TABLESPACE test_data ONLINE;
```

3) LOSS OF DATA FILE OF TABLESPACE SYSTEM

The database cannot be opened without this presence of the tablespace, the recovery will be made base in MOUNT state.

a) The view V$RECOVER_FILE shows the file

```
SQL > SELECT * FROM V$RECOVER_FILE ;
```
The data file 1 is to recover. Put OFFLINE
ALTER DATABASE DATAFILE 1 OFFLINE;
(Not required as the database is MOUNTED)

b) Restore the lost file.

```
SQL > HOST COPY C: \SAVE_DATA\System01.dbf
C: \ oracle \ oradata \ demo
```

c) Recover lost file after verifying the archives required.

```
SQL > RECOVER DATAFILE 1 ;
```

d) set the data file ONLINE.

(if it was OFFLINE)
```
SQL > ALTER Database datafile 1 online;
```

E) Open the database

```
SQL > ALTER DATABASE OPEN ;
```

▶ **Caution:**

During the recovery of data files or the entire database, the automatic application of logs can be done in three ways:

1) By the SQL * PLUS
   ```
   SQL > SET AUTORECOVERY ON before starting the
   recovery
   ```

2) By use of the clause AUTOMATIC in the command RECOVER
   ```
   SQL > RECOVER AUTOMATIC datafile |database ....
   ```

3) In entering AUTO to the question asked by
   ```
   Specify {<RET> = suggested | filename | AUTO |
   CANCEL}
   ```

If any of these three ways is not chosen, the recovery is manual. What may be long, when many archives are applied.

II-1-B-2—INCOMPLETE RECOVERY

PRESENTATION

The incomplete recovery rebuilds the database to a point in time before failure. The data generated after that point in time are lost and must be reentered manually. We should use this type of recovery that is performed database closed in case of absolute necessity.
Prior, we must have the followings:

- A Backup of all data files
- All files from the archivelog until time specified for recovery.
- And in some cases a copy of control file.

Situations requiring an incomplete recovery are:

- Failed to complete recovery because of the lack of an archive redo logfile

- Loss of current log file
- Loss of all control files
- User errors (deletion of a table or a tablespace, validation of incorrect updates in a table).

There are three types of incomplete recovery:

- Recovery to a point in time
  This type of recovery must be used when the date and approximate time of user error or loss of a log file is known.

For example:
A user indicates you to have validated updates or deleted an important table at an approximate time. This time can be obtained using LogMiner or flashback tool. The entire database is then brought back to this hour.

- Recovery until cancel
  This type of recovery must be used if

- The current log file is lost
- An archive needed for recovery is no longer available
  It ends when CANCEL responds to the request specification name of log file.

- Recovery based on the SCN
  This type of recovery ends when all the changes to the number (not included) SCN (System Change Number) specified has been validated.

NOTE: The syntax in this type of recovery is
SQL>RECOVER .... UNTIL CHANGE scn

Steps to follow

It is strongly recommended to follow the steps below when an incomplete recovery in done:

1) Perform a whole database offline backup (data files, Redo Log files and control files) to another location. This is very important to be able to resume the recovery in case of failure of the previous. An error by the DBA in the case example of specifying a mistake time of recovery may be fatal if the total backup has not been performed.
2) Consult the dynamic performance views and the ALERT file as in the case of complete recovery
3) Restore all data files (<u>never restore the Redo Log files</u>). Control files can be restored only if we want to recover with an old control file.
4) Ensure that the archived logs required for recovery are availiable.
5) Apply the command RECOVER DATABASE . . . . (Done at the state MOUNT)
6) Open the database with RESETLOGS option
   ```
   SQL> ALTER DATABASE OPEN RESETLOGS ;
   ```
7) Make a new whole database backup, database closed (is no longer necessary since the 10g version, old backups can be reused)
8) No longer needed to save the LOG file archives to a new location and then delete to avoid the system mixing records from different incarnations of the database. ; The incarnation number present in the parameter LOG_ARCHIVE_FORMAT (in versions 10g and later) differentiates the logs from different incarnations.
9) Open the database.

▶ **Caution:**

```
Before recovery, you must check the view V$RECOVER_
FILE if files to be recovered are OFFLINE, if so put
them ONLINE. Otherwise they may be permanently lost
after the execution of the RECOVER DATABASE and ALTER
DATABASE OPEN RESETLOGS commands.
```

Examples of incomplete recovery

1) Validation error in a table

A user accidentally executes:
```
SQL >UPDATE Scott.emp Set ename = 'TEST';
SQL >COMMIT;
```

At the approximate date 30/09/2004 at 10:05: 10
Since no file is damaged or lost, the view V$Recovery_log contains no rows.
Proceed as follows:

    a) SQL > SHUTDOWN IMMEDIATE ;
          Then make a total backup of the database to another location
    b) Restore all data files

Sample script Restoration

```
COPY C:\save_data\SYSTEM01.DBF C:\oracle\oradata\DEMO
COPY C:\save_data\RBS01.DBF C:\oracle\oradata\DEMO
COPY C:\save_data\USERS01.DBF C:\oracle\oradata\DEMO
COPY C:\save_data\TEMP01.DBF C:\oracle\oradata\DEMO
COPY C:\save_data\TOOLS01.DBF C:\oracle\oradata\DEMO
COPY C:\save_data\INDX01.DBF C:\oracle\oradata\DEMO
COPY C:\save_data\DR01.DBF C:\oracle\oradata\DEMO
COPY C:\save_data\OEM_REPOSITORY.ORA C:\oracle\
oradata/DEMO
```

    c) Recovery of the database up to the time of the error
          SQL >RECOVER DATABASE UNTIL TIME '2004-09-30 10:05:00' ;
    d) Open the database with a new incarnation
          SQL > ALTER DATABASE OPEN RESETLOGS;
    e) Stop the instance
          SQL > SHUTDOWN IMMEDIATE ;
    f) Perform a total backup of the database
    g) Open the database
          SQL > STARTUP;

In a session SQL * Plus, we check that the table scott. emp has been restored to its state before the error.

```
SQL > SELECT ENAME FROM SCOTT.emp
```

2) Loss of the current log file

Simulation

- **a** – multiplication of employees' salaries by 10, stop the database and loss of the current log file.
- **b** – **SQL > UPDATE Scott.emp Set sal = sal * 10;**
  ```
  SQL> COMMIT;
  SQL> SHUTDOWN IMMEDIATE
  ```

At the the instance startup, the database cannot be opened in the absence of the current log file

- **c** – Consult V$LOG view to determine the sequence number corresponding to the current log
- **d** – Restore all data files
- **e** – Check status of data files (put online those who are offline before the recovery)
  SQL > SELECT file#, status FROM V$datafile_header;
- **f** – Recover the database with the option UNTIL CANCEL
  SQL > RECOVER DATABASE UNTIL CANCEL;

After applying the last sequence number preceding the current corresponding log, respond CANCEL.

Consultation the Sal column of the table Scott.emp displays the initial amounts (before the increase in wages by 10).
The update has been applied in the current log and it has not been archived before the loss.

3) Deleting a tablespace accidentally

Scenario: a tablespace has been accidentally deleted

SQL > DROP TABLESPACE example INCLUDING CONTENTS;

An examination of the alert file gives us the date and time of removal (by 14.10.2004 at 15: 10: 33)

Extract of alert File

LGWR: Primary database is in. CLUSTER CONSISTENT mode
Opened log thread 1 sequence at a
Current log # 1 seq # a member # 0:
C: \ oracle \ oradata \ test9 \ REDO01.LOG
Successful open of redo thread 1.
Thu 14 October 2004 2:47:05 p.m.
SMON: enabling cache recovery
Thu 14 October 2004 2:47:08 p.m.
Undo Segment 1 Onlined
Undo Segment 2 Onlined
Undo Segment 3 Onlined
Undo Segment 4 Onlined
Undo Segment 5 Onlined
Undo Segment 6 Onlined
Undo Segment 7 Onlined
Undo Segment 8 Onlined
Undo Segment 9 Onlined
Undo Segment 10 Onlined
Successfully onlined Undo Tablespace 1.
Thu 14 October 2004 2:47:08 p.m.
SMON: enabling tx recovery
Thu 14 October 2004 2:47:08 p.m.
Database characterset IS WE8ISO8859P1
replication_dependency_tracking Turned off (no async multimaster replication found)
Completed: alter database open
Thu 14 October 2004 3:07:32 p.m.
drop tablespace example including contents
Thu 14 October 2004 3:07:33 p.m.
ORA-23515 signalled During: Drop tablespace example including contents ...
Thu 14 October 2004 3:10:21 p.m.

The backup control file (made before the deletion) contains information on the tablespace. The recovery of this tablespace will therefore be done with the use of the copy control file, follow these steps:

a) Stop the database and then save the control file (s) to a new location for safety reasons
b) Restore all the datafiles and control file backup
c) An attempt to open the database returns an error message
d) Check for file offline by select * from V$Recover_file and put them online
e) Recover the database
    ```
    SQL > RECOVER DATABASE UNTIL TIME
    '2004-10-14 15:10:00' USING BACKUP CONTROLFILE
    ```
f) Open the database with a new incarnation
    ```
    SQL > ALTER DATABASE OPEN RESETLOGS;
    ```
g) Stop the database and do a whole database backup

II-2 BACKUP & RECOVERY MANAGED BY RMAN

II-2.a BACKUP MANAGED BY RECOVERY MANAGER (RMAN)

PRESENTATION OF RMAN

Recovery Manager (RMAN) is an Oracle utility available from the **Version 8** to manage backup, restoration and data recovery.

▶ **Caution:**

```
Since Oracle 10g version, you can still use the
user-managed backups. But if something goes wrong,
you can't receive technical support from Oracle,
where the need now to use RMAN.
```

RMAN offers many features that are not available when performing backups and restores managed by the user. Some are:

- Copy of the only blocks occupied during the backup
- Possibility to limit the size of the backup to only blocks changed since the last backup using incremental backups to block level
- Possibility to parallelize backups
- Ability to plan RMAN operations as scheduled tasks
- possibility to enable database blok change tracking for faster incremental backups
- Possibility to store the current operations in form of scripts

RECOVERY Manager Components
RMAN is composed of:

- RMAN executable to call the command line interface
- OEM: for launch RMAN in Oracle Enterprise Manager.
- Server Sessions: The server processes or threads called by RMAN Enterprise Manager Graphic connect to target database to execute the backup / restore /and recovery options via an interface PL/SQL
- Target Database: database being the backed up / restored
- Repository RMAN: data used by RMAN for these operations (called metadata) are stored in control files of the target database and possibly in the database catalog restoration called recovery catalog.
- Channel: for backup and recovery, RMAN uses a channel for its connection to the database
- MML (Media Management Library) library used by RMAN for access to tape. Since 10g version, we can use Oracle Secure Backup to both make tape backups as backup files that are not Oracle files

Types of databases used by RMAN

RMAN can use three types of databases:

- Target Database
- Recovery catalog database
- Auxiliary Database

a) Connection without recovery catalog

The target database is the base for which you want to perform a backup / recovery.
Example:

```
$ rman TARGET user/pass_word@service_name
                    Or
$ export ORACLE_SID=orcl
$ rman TARGET /
```

In this case, information relating to the backup file is stored in the target database control file.

b) Connecting with recovery catalog

The recovery catalog is a basic knowledge of RMAN. It consists of a set of tables, views, indexes and packages . . . It is optional and contains information on:

- The data files and backup sets of data files and archives
- Copies of data files
- Archived redo logfiles
- The stored scripts
- The physical structure of the target database.

☞ **NB:** The information on backups are also stored in the controlfile of the target database, but they are kept longer in the recovery catalog.

It is updated when performing one of the following:

- Registering the target database in the catalog
- Resync the catalog with the control file of the target database
- Restoring the incarnation of the database
- Modification of information containing backups or files
- Perform a backup, restore or recovery

The use of the catalog is recommended in the following cases:

- use of stored scripts
- Centralized management of multiple databases.
- Keeping long-term backups

☞ **NB**: The version of the recovery catalog should be at least equal to that of RMAN client. Otherwise proceed with the upgrade of the catalog.

```
$rman [TARGET sys/oracle@targetdb] catalog urman/
urman@rcvcat
RMAN>UPGRADE CATALOG;
RMAN>=== confirmation message
RMAN>UPGRADE CATALOG;
```

```
After creating the catalog (see next step) the
launch of RMAN would require (eg Windows):
C: > RMAN Target sys/password@name_service_bd
RCVCAT rman/rman@name_ser_cat
```

Creating a recovery catalog

1) Creating a tablespace
   In the database containing the recovery catalog, create a tablespace
2) Create a user catalog.
3) Grant Privileges and roles to manage the recovery catalog to this user.
4) in the OS, run the command to connect to catalog and create it.
5) Under the operating system, connection to the target database with the recovery catalog previously created
6) Register the target database in the catalog

Before beginning any backup / restore/recover operation, the database must be registered in the catalog, if not the storage information on this database will not be made. This is done by the command

```
RMAN>REGISTER DATABASE;
```

The command register database resynchronizes catalog with the control file. Synchronization is done automatically during BACKUP or COPY, setting tablespace off or Online. It must be done manually by running the command

```
RMAN>RESYNC CATALOG
```

after completing one of the followings:

- Adding, Deleting a tablespace
- Adding, deleting a data file
- Moving a file in the database

Sample of catalog creation

```
====================================
= CREATION catalog in DB 11g
====================================


$export ORACLE_SID=orcl11g
$sqlplus / as sysdba
SQL>create tablespace RCAT_TS datafile '/u01/app/
oracle/oradata/orcl11g/rcat01.dbf' size 50M
autoextend on next 1M maxsize unlimited;
SQL>create user urman identified by urman default
tablespace rcat_ts quota unlimited
on rcat_ts;
SQL>grant recovery_catalog_owner to urman;
SQL> exit
$ rman catalog urman /urman
RMAN>create catalog;
RMAN>exit;
```

[Oracle @ server1 ~] $ rman target sys /oracle@orcl rcvcat urman/urman@orcl11g
Recovery Manager: Release 10.2.0.1.0—Production on Tue January 23 2010 5:08:36 p.m.
Copyright (c) 1982, 2005, Oracle. All rights reserved.

connected to target database: ORCL (DBID = 1226910228)
connected to recovery catalog database
RMAN>register database;
database registered in recovery catalog
starting full resync of recovery catalog
full resync complete.

RMAN>list incarnation;
List of Database Incarnations
DB Key Inc Key DB Name DB ID STATUS Reset SCN Reset Time

| -- | --- | ------- | ------------ | -------------------- | ------------ |
| 1 | 18 | ORCL | 1226910228 | PARENT 1 | 30-JUN-05 |
| 1 | 2 | ORCL | 1226910228 | CURRENT 446075 | 01-OCT-09 |

RMAN>

c) Connection to an auxiliary instance

The auxiliary instance is used for operations such as replications (We'll discuss this concept in detail later in this book)

$ rman TARGET /
RMAN>connect auxiliary user/pwd@auxdb

RMAN COMMANDS

The RMAN commands can be classified into two types:

- autonomous commands
- work commands

The autonomous commands are self-executed commands at the prompt RMAN and cannot be included in a RUN block. Examples are:

```
CREATE CATALOG, RESYNC CATALOG, CHANGE, CONNECT,
{CREATE | DELETE | REPLACE |LIST } SCRIPT, SET DBID
```

Work commands are executed in block and should be inside a block RUN (between the braces ({and}). If an error occurs on a order, the rest is abandoned.
Example: Allocate channel

```
RUN {ALLOCATE CHANNEL C1 TYPE DISK
FORMAT = 'C:\SAVE_RMAN\%u';
BACKUP DATAFILE 'C:\DEMO_DATA \data01.dbf' ; }
```

There are mixed commands that can be undertaken individually or placed inside a block of work: e.g

```
RMAN>backup tablespace users;
                 or
RMAN>RUN>{ backup tablespace users; }
```

EXECUTION OF RMAN COMMANDS

RMAN commands can be submitted into two ways :

1) –Interactively at the RMAN prompt
   `RMAN>BACKUP DATABASE;`
2) –In Batch mode by saving a series of command into a file and launching it by using @ Or @@
   $rman TARGET /
   RMAN>@ my_backupdb.rman

☞ If the file you execute contains a call to another file, this call must be done using @@

Sample
File mybacup.rman contains :

```
    backup tablespace users;
    backup datafile 2;
    @@/home/oracle/backup_log.rman
```

File backup_log.rman contains :

```
backup archivelog all;

You can launch by :
$ rman TARGET /
RMAN>@/home/oracle/mybackup.rman
            Or
$rman target / CMDFILE=/home/oracle/mybackup.rman
```

SAMPLE OF SOME FEW COMMANDS

Allocation channel command

Before any backup / restore by RMAN, a channel must be allocated in advance. There is a default preconfigured disk channel. The allocation is done manually by the ALLOCATE command which simplified syntax is:

```
RMAN > RUN {ALLOCATE CHANNEL channel_name
TYPE {DISK |TAPE} FORMAT = 'Path/type_format';}
```

The type of format in general can be

%c	Indicates the copy number of the element in a backup set whose elements are split
%p	Indicates the element number in the backup set. This value starts at 1 for each backup set and increases by increments of 1 to each element of backing up creation.
%s	Indicates the number of backup set. This number is a counter in the control file, which increases for each backup set.
%d	Indicates the name of the database.
%n	Specifies the name of the database, right-padded with characters x to reach a total length of 8 characters.
%t	Indicates the timestamp of the backup set, a 4-byte value got from the number of seconds since a fixed reference time. The combination of %s and %t can be used to form a unique name for the backup set.

%u	Indicates an 8-character name consisting of compressed representations of the backup set number and time of its creation.
%U	Specifies a convenient shorthand for % u_% p_% c that guarantees uniqueness of the backup file names generated.

☞ **Example:**
```
RMAN > RUN {ALLOCATE CHANNEL C1 TYPE DISK FORMAT
= 'C:\SAVE_RMAN\%s%t';}
```

▶ **Remark**

If the format name is not specified, RMAN uses %U by default. Make the difference between %u and %U (lowercase and uppercase)

If the specified channel was previously allocated, it is unassigned and assigned to the new specified. For the channel to be used by a subsequent command (Eg BACKUP),it must be in the block because the channel is released at the end of the execution of the block if not "persistent" (see CONFIGURE command).

➢ **BACKUP command**
The BACKUP command can back up to disk or on tape:

- Data files, archived logs
- Tablespaces
- The entire database

With the possibility to include the control file. The backup on disk can be saved on tape.

☞ **Examples:**
1) RMAN > BACKUP DATABASE [FORCE] [TAG = 'Beacon_ name'] ; Option FORCE used to back up objects which contents equal to the backup even if optimization mode is enabled.

If the Tag is not specified, a default tag based on timestamp will be assigned. To better follow your backups, you can use your own tags. During restore, you issue e.g.
Restore..From TAG = 'Beacon_name'

2) Back up sets to tape backups that were created more than five days and delete them on disk
RMAN>BACKUP DEVICE TYPE SBT BACKUP SET CREATED BEFORE SYSDATE-5 DELETE INPUT;

3) Backup of a tablespace
RMAN > BACKUP TABLESPACE DEMO_DATA ;

➢ COPY Command

The command copy makes an image copy of file. The output file is always on a disk. Data files and archives can be copied. The copied files being the binary image of the source files, they can be directly used in a recovery without having to be restored.

☞ **Example:**

```
RMAN > COPY DATAFILE 1 TO 'C : \SAVE_RMAN\
data1. dbf',
DATAFILE 2 TO 'C : \Save_RMAN\data2. dbf',
ARCHIVELOG 'C : \archives\Demo81711.zip' TO
'C: \SAVE_RMAN\Arc81711.bak';
```

➢ CONFIGURE command

The CONFIGURE command permits to configure parameters for permanent work Backup / Restoration and maintenance of RMAN. The values assigned to these parameters remain unchanged for all sessions until they are redefined. This command can be used for:

- Configure automatic channels
- Specify the backup retention policy
- Specify the number of backup copies to create
- Limit the size of backup sets
- Exclude a tablespace from backup

- Enable / disable backup optimization
- Automatically save or not the control file during a backup of a data file.
- Set the encryption algorithm
- Set the compression algorithm
- Configure the conservation of archived logs

☞ Examples:

```
RMAN>CONFIGURE CHANNEL DEVICE TYPE DISK FORMAT =
'C\SAVE_RMAN\%U';
RMAN>CONFIGURE RETENTION POLICY TO REDUNDANCY 6 ;
RMAN>CONFIGURE RETENTION POLICY TO RECOVERY WINDOW
OF 5 days;
RMAN>CONFIGURE Exclude FOR TABLESPACE test;
Excludes tablespace test from backup
```
(All tablespaces except SYSTEM can be excluded. But an explicit backup command of this tablespace saves the tablespace).
```
RMAN>RUN {BACKUP TABLESPACE test ;}
RMAN>CONFIGURE BACKUP OPTIMIZATION ON;
```
Optimization prevents RMAN from backing up a file to a device type if the identical file is already backed up on this device.

```
RMAN>CONFIGURE ARCHIVELOG DELETION POLICY TO BACKED
UP 2 TIMES to sbt;
RMAN>Configure compression algorithm 'BZIP2';
RMAN>Configure encryption algorithm 'AES192';
```

```
Use the CLEAR option to restore the default values.
```

☞ **Example:**

```
To return this tablespace in the backup strategy, run:
RMAN>CONFIGURE Exclude FOR TABLESPACE test CLEAR;
You can also use the option NOEXECLUDE in the command
Backup to back up tablespaces previously exempted
RMAN>BACKUP NOEXECLUDE DATABASE;
```

➢ SHOW command

The SHOW command displays the persistent configuration parameters specified using the CONFIGURE command

☞ **Example:**

```
RMAN >SHOW ALL;
RMAN > SHOW RETENTION POLICY;
```

➢ LIST Command

Generates a detailed report containing information on:

- Backup sets
- Copies of files

☞ Example:

```
RMAN>LIST BACKUP OF DATABASE ;
```

➢ REPORT Command

Provides detailed analysis of the informations related to the repository of Recovery Manager.

☞ **Example:**

```
RMAN>REPORT NEEDS BACKUP;
Displays all data files requiring backup
RMAN>REPORT OBSOLETE;
Displays all backup files which are obsolete according
to the retention rule;
RMAN>REPORT SCHEMA;
Displays the structure of the target database;
Maintenance operations can be performed using enterprise Manager.
```

Backup Settings with Enterprise Manager

ORACLE Enterprise Manager 11g
Database Control

Database Instance: orcl11g.oracle.com >

Backup Settings

Device | Backup Set | Policy

Backup Policy

☑ Automatically backup the control file and server parameter file (SPFILE) with every backup and database structural change

Autobackup Disk Location

An existing directory or diskgroup name where the control file and server parameter file will be backed up. If you do not specify a location, the files will be backed up to the flash recovery area location.

☑ Optimize the whole database backup by skipping unchanged files such as read-only and offline datafiles that have been backed up

☑ Enable block change tracking for faster incremental backups

Block Change Tracking File /u01/app/oracle/oradata/orcl11g/track_f|

Specify a location and file, otherwise an Oracle managed file will be created in the database area.

Tablespaces Excluded From Whole Database Backup

Populate this table with the tablespaces you want to exclude from a whole database backup. Use the Add button to add tablespaces to this table.

(Add)

Select Tablespace Name	Tablespace Number	Status	Contents
No Items Selected			

☑ TIP These tablespaces can be backed up separately using tablespace backup.

Retention Policy

○ Retain All Backups

You must manually delete any backups

● Retain backups that are necessary for a recovery to any time within the specified number of days (point-in-time recovery)   Days 2

Recovery Window

○ Retain at least the specified number of full backups for each datafile   Backups 1

Redundancy

Archivelog Deletion Policy

Backups retention policy

A retention policy describes the backups that will be retained and for how long.

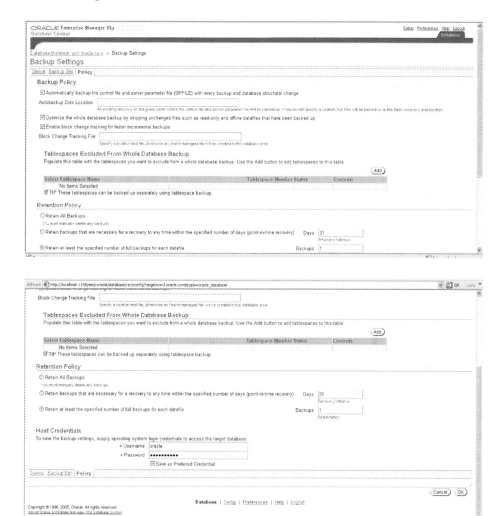

The RMAN CONFIGURE command can define two types of retention rules mutually exclusive:

- Windows Recovery
- Redundancy

Retention policy with window recovery

This policy is defined by the number of days. For each data file, it must always exist in the view v$backup_files at least one backup satisfying the following condition:
SYSDATE—COMPLETION _TIME > = recovery window

☞ **Example:** recovery Window of 5 days

```
RMAN>CONFIGURE RETENTION POLICY TO RECOVERY WINDOW
OF 5 days;
```

The value shown ensures that a recovery till the number of days in time will always be possible. Backups prior to this number are considered obsolete, if there is at least one posterior and outside the window of recovery

If you do not have a recovery catalog, the recovery window must be less than or equal to the value of initialization parameter CONTROL_FILE_RECORD_KEEP_TIME to avoid replacing the oldest backups in the control file. However, if you use a catalog, make sure the parameter CONTROL_FILE_RECORD_KEEP_TIME exceeds the interval between resynchronizations catalog.

Retention policy with redundancy

This policy defines the number of copies of backups kept. Backups exceeding this number are considered obsolete.

☞ **Example:** Conservation Strategy 2 copies of backup file

```
RMAN>CONFIGURE RETENTION POLICY TO REDUNDANCY 2;
```

▶ **Caution:**

• The SQL/SQL+ commands can be executed in RMAN. Except SQL statements requiring SYSDBA privilege such as STARTUP, MOUNT, RECOVER, the SQL statements allowed by RMAN must be preceded by SQL.

Example:

```
Setting a tablespace offline
RMAN>SQL 'ALTER TABLESPACE DEMO_DATA OFFLINE';
```

- The FETCH are not made in RMAN, then a SELECT statement will not show any results.

MANAGING SCRIPTS

RMAN script is a set of commands defining the backup, restore and recovery operations the most frequently used. It is stored in the recovery catalog and can be scheduled as a job.

Since 10g versions, a script can be global; in this case it is accessible to all registered databases.

The script is managed by the commands:

a) Create a script

```
RMAN>CREATE [GLOBAL] SCRIPT script_name {
List of commands RMAN } COMMENT ='comment';
                Or
RMAN>CREATE [GLOBAL] SCRIPT script_name FROM
'file_name'
COMMENT ='comment';
```

b) Replace a script

```
RMAN>REPLACE [GLOBAL] SCRIPT script_name {
                Or
RMAN>REPLACE [GLOBAL] SCRIPT script_name FROM
'file_name'
COMMENT ='comment';
```

All the existing lines need to be rewritten; if the script does not exist it is created.

c) Delete a script

```
RMAN>DELETE [GLOBAL] SCRIPT script_name
```

d) List scripts

```
RMAN>LIST [ALL | GLOBAL} SCRIPT NAMES
List the names of all scripts stored in the
catalog. ALL clause, the default option lists
both global and local scripts, thus needs to be
connected to the target database to use that
option.
```

e) Print a script

```
RMAN>PRINT [GLOBAL] SCRIPT script_name [TO FILE
'file_name'];
```

f) Execute a script

```
RMAN>RUN        {EXECUPTE        [GLOBAL]        SCRIPT
script_name;}
```

Caution:

- RMAN does not have a text editor, it is advisable to update your scripts using a text editor and load it with RMAN>{CREATE | REPLACE} SCRIPT FROM 'file_name';
- The names of the script are case sensitive.
- A Local script can have the same name than a Global script
- In 11g versions, you can specify parameters (&n) when creating or updating a script. These parameters are prompting during the creation of the script and can be substituted during the execution.

SAMPLE OF USAGE OF A SCRIPT

```
[oracle@server1 ~]$ rman target sys/oracle@orcl

Recovery Manager: Release 10.2.0.3.0—Production on
Sun Oct 17 14:09:27 2010

Copyright (c) 1982, 2005, Oracle. All rights
reserved.

connected to target database: ORCL
(DBID=1226910228)
RMAN>connect catalog rman/rman@orcl11g

RMAN-04007: WARNING from recovery catalog database:
ORA-28002: the password will expire within 7 days

connected to recovery catalog database

RMAN>create script daily_backup {

backup format = '/u02/app/oracle/database/
backup_orcl/%U'
(database include current controlfile);
backup (archivelog all delete input);
}2> 3> 4> 5> 6>

created script daily_backup
```

 — **The name of the script is case sensitive**

```
RMAN>print script Daily_backup;

RMAN-00571:
=====================================================
RMAN-00569: =========== ERROR MESSAGE STACK FOLLOWS
==============
RMAN-00571:
```

```
==========================================================
RMAN-06004: ORACLE error from recovery catalog
database: RMAN-20400: stored script not found
RMAN-06083: error when loading stored script
Daily_backup

RMAN>print script daily_backup;
printing stored script: daily_backup
{backup format = '/u01/app/oracle/database/
backup_orcl/%U'
(database include current controlfile);
backup (archivelog all delete input);
}
----------------------------------------------------------
```

To Launch the script, type :

```
----------------------------------------------------------
RMAN>run {execute script daily_backup;}

executing script: daily_backup

Starting backup at 17-OCT-10
allocated channel: ORA_DISK_1
channel ORA_DISK_1: sid=145 devtype=DISK
channel ORA_DISK_1: starting full datafile backupset
channel ORA_DISK_1: specifying datafile(s) in backupset
input datafile fno=00001 name=/u01/app/oracle/
oradata/orcl/system01.dbf
input datafile fno=00002 name=/u01/app/oracle/
oradata/orcl/undotbs01.dbf
input datafile fno=00003 name=/u01/app/oracle/
oradata/orcl/sysaux01.dbf
input datafile fno=00005 name=/u01/app/oracle/
oradata/orcl/example01.dbf
input datafile fno=00006 name=/u01/app/oracle/
oradata/orcl/lgmnr_tbs01.dbf
input datafile fno=00004 name=/u01/app/oracle/
oradata/orcl/users01.dbf
channel ORA_DISK_1: starting piece 1 at 17-OCT-10
```

II-2-b. RECOVERY MANAGED BY RMAN

The RMAN recovery is performed following the same principles as the recovery managed by the user. We present below a case of complete recovery and a case of incomplete recovery.

a) Complete recovery

The DBA has created a tablespace test and has put a copy of the customer file. The data file is on a disk (simulated here by C: \ repert_defect) that fails and no backup was made.

The recovery of this tablespace is still possible following the same path as the recovery managed by the user. We assume that the disk was damaged when the database was closed.

▶ **Caution:**

The SELECT statement displaying no line under RMAN, another session is to be opened in conjunction with RMAN to consult the views mentioned in the user-managed recovery (V$RECOVER_FILE, V$Datafile_header . . .). 1 **SQL>Select file#, status, error from V$datafile_header;** confirms that the file number 16 is missing and its status is ONLINE

1) Place the data file offline
   RMAN>SQL 'alter database datafile 16 offline';
2) Open the database
   RMAN>ALTER DATABASE OPEN;
3) Assign a new location in data file 16
   RMAN>RUN {SET NEWNAME FOR DATAFILE 16
   TO 'C: \repert_new\data.dbf';}
4) Register the new file location in the control file
   RMAN>RUN {SWITCH DATAFILE 16 ;}
5) Recover the lost tablespace
   RMAN>RECOVER TABLESPACE test ;
6) Set the tablespace Online
   RMAN>SQL 'Alter TABLESPACE test online';

b) Incomplete Recovery

With RMAN, we can use, the followings modes:

- UNTIL TIME
- UNTIL SCN
- UNTIL SEQUENCE
- UNTIL RESTORE POINT (starting from 10g version)

Note that we can't specify UNTIL CANCEL by RMAN, while here we have UNTIL SEQUENCE which is not present using recovery managed by user. The recovery is performed until the target point specified (not included). The backup of the database before this point must be available otherwise an error will be generated.

Scenario
A user updates the table customer by mistake. You determine the approximate time 13.10.2004 at 17.10.
Proceed as follows:

1) Start the database in MOUNT state
2) Set the date and time of stopping the recovery point by the command

```
RMAN > RUN {SET UNTIL TIME '2004-10-13 17:10:00';}
```

 Caution:

The date format must be compatible with the format of the environment variable NLS_DATE_FORMAT which also depends on NLS_LANG
In our example, affect this variable (under Windows):
C:> SET NLS_DATE_FORMAT='YYYY-MM-DD HH24:MI:SS'

3) Restore the database

```
RMAN>RESTORE DATABASE;
```

4) Recover the database

```
RMAN > RECOVER DATABASE;
```

5) Open the database with a new incarnation

```
RMAN > ALTER DATABASE OPEN RESETLOGS;
```

Use a block of work for all that commands :

```
RUN {
SET UNTIL TIME = '2004-10-13 17:10:00';
RESTORE DATABASE ;
RECOVER DATABASE ;
ALTER DATABASE OPEN RESETLOGS; }
```

6) If recovery is made in mode nocatalog, register the new incarnation in the catalog before you can use it with the command

```
RMAN > RESET DATABASE;
```

7) Make a new backup of the database.

OTHER RECOVERY SCENARIOS

a) Loss of non-current logs.

Redo logfiles of the database may be in the main following states (state got by consulting the column STATUS of the V$log view)

- CURRENT The file is in use by the LGWR process
- ACTIVE The file is not in use but it is necessary for instance recovery
- INACTIVE The file is not in use and is no longer necessary for instance recovery.

- UNUSED The file has not been used, it is the case if it has been added recently.
- CLEARING the file is truncated (by SQL>ALTER DATABASE CLEAR LOGFILE).

In case of loss of a log that is not current, it is enough to recreate the lost file by the command

```
SQL> ALTER DATABASE CLEAR UNARCHIVED LOGFILE 'filename';
                              or
SQL>ALTER DATABASE CLEAR UNARCHIVED LOGFILE GROUP
no_gpe;
```

Before this command, ensure that the status of the file is neither CURRENT nor ACTIVE.
If this is not the case, proceed first to a switch logfile

```
SQL> ALTER SYSTEM SWITCH LOGFILE;
```

If the files are multiplexed redo logfiles, the loss of members of the current log does not require the incomplete recovery if it remains at least one.
In this case proceed as before after a switch logfile.

b) Loss of control file.

In case of loss of all control files, the database cannot be mounted. You must make a recovery from backup as follows: (eg with RMAN);

```
$export ORACLE_SID=orcl
$rman target /
RMAN>STARTUP NOMOUNT;
RMAN>SET DBID NO_dbid;
RMAN>RESTORE CONTROLFILE FROM AUTOBACKUP;
RMAN>ALTER DATABASE MOUNT;
RMAN>RECOVER DATABASE;
RMAN>ALTER DATABASE OPEN RESETLOGS;
```

The command SET DBID is required if you are not using a recovery catalog.

c) Recovery from an image copy

Backups as image copies can be used directly in a recovery operation without restoration. Suppose that file n (file number in the V$datafile view) is lost and previously was saved as a copy (BACKUP AS COPY)

```
RMAN>SQL 'ALTER DATABASE DATAFILE n OFFLINE';
RMAN>SWITCH DATAFILE n TO COPY;
RMAN>RECOVER DATAFILE n;
RMAN>SQL 'ALTER DATABASE DATAFILE n ONLINE';
```

d) Block recover

When there are physical corruptions in some bocks of a datafile, you can proceed to a block recover since version 9i instead of restoring the whole file and then perform a recovery.
The benefits of this type of recovery are;

- The datafile is online during recovery
- Only the faulty blocks being recovered are unavailable during the operation

RMAN uses complete recovery mechanism to do that operation by:

- Identifying the backups from which the blocks will recovered
- Read the backups in chronological order till it find a safe block. You can use UNTIL option to limit the backups to read
- Starts the restoration of the blocs accumulated and then perform the recovery operation

Samples of simplified syntaxes

```
1) RMAN>BLOCKRECOVER DATAFILE n BLOCK b1,..., bn
   [DATAFILE p BLACK p1,..., pn]
   [RESTORE UNTIL clause];
```

If until clause is time, the value of time must be specified between 'and'

2) RMAN>BLOCRECOVER CORRUPTION LIST RESTORE UNTIL 'sysdate-2';
To recover all corrupted blocks in the database (listed in V$database_block_corruption view) with the scope of the backup limited to the backups done before 2 days.

<New 11 g>
On version 11g, the syntax BLOCKRECOVER has been replaced by RMAN>RECOVER ... BLOCK ...

II-3 FLASH REVOVERY AREA (FRA)

The FLASH REVOVERY AREA, introduced in Oracle version 10g is an area on disk where are by default stored backups of data files and archived logs. It may also contain archived logs, automatic backup controlfile, the tracking modified blocks file, flashback logs.

Configuration of the flash recovery area

The configuration of this area is made using two initialization parameters (dynamic).

- DB_RECOVERY_FILE_DEST_SIZE which indicates the size
- DB_RECOVERY_FILE_DEST that specifies its location

```
SQL> Alter system set db_recovery_file_dest_size = 5G;
(The size setting must be done first).
SQL> alter system set db_recovery_file_dest = '/u01/
app oracle/ FRA';
SQL> alter system set db_ecovery_file_dest = '+FRA';
(If using ASM files)
When creating the database by DBCA, a recovery area
by default is proposed with a size of 2GB.
```

☞ **NB.:** During the allocation of this area, there is no verification of the actual space available. You must ensure in advance the space available especially when you use an ASM disk group as FRA for not having a backup error for lack of space, while the size of your backups is less than the size of the FRA but not real.

THE CONFIGURATION CAN ALSO BE DONE THROUGH ENTERPRISE MANAGER

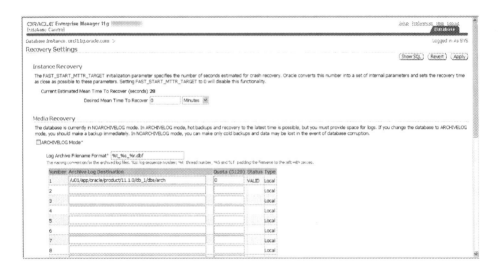

9				Local
10	USE_DB_RECOVERY_FILE_DEST	n/a	VALID	Local

☑ TIP It is recommended that archive log files be written to multiple locations spread across two different disks.
☑ TIP You can specify up to 10 archive log destinations.

Flash Recovery

Flash Recovery Area is enabled for this database. The chart shows space used by each file type that is not reclaimable by Oracle. Performing backups to a tertiary storage is one way to make space reclaimable. Usable Flash Recovery Area includes free and reclaimable space.

Flash Recovery Area Usage

Flash Recovery Area Location /u01/app/oracle/flash_recovery_area

Flash Recovery Area Size 2 [GB]

Flash Recovery Area Size must be set when the location is set.

Reclaimable Flash Recovery Area (B) 0

Free Flash Recovery Area (GB) 0

☐ Enable Flashback Database - flashback logging can be used for fast database point-in-time recovery"
The fast recovery area must be set to enable flashback logging. When using flashback logs, you may recover your entire database to a prior point-in-time without restoring files. Flashback is the preferred point-in-time recovery method in the recovery wizard when appropriate.

Flashback Retention Time 24 [Hours]

Current size of the flashback logs(GB) n/a

Lowest SCN in the flashback data n/a

Flashback Time n/a

■ CONTROL FILE – 0GB (0%)
■ REDO LOG – 0GB (0%)
■ ARCHIVED LOG – 0GB (0%)
■ BACKUP PIECE – 0GB (0%)
■ IMAGE COPY – 0GB (0%)
■ FLASHBACK LOG – 0GB (0%)
■ Usable – 2GB (100%)

☐ Apply changes to SPFILE only. Otherwise the changes will be made to both SPFILE and the running instance which requires that you restart the database to invoke static parameters.

☑ TIP * indicates controls, if changed, must restart database to invoke.

(Show SQL) (Revert) (Apply)

Database | Setup | Preferences | Help | Logout

Advantages of the Flash Recovery Area

The use of the flash recovery area as the location of backup offers great flexibility:

- The backup scripts do not have to be modified if the location of this area is changed.
- The backup files obsolete according to the retention policy are automatically deleted when space is required in this area.

However, the following elements can't be placed in this area:

- The snapshot control file
- Backups to keep forever

Backup of the Flash Recovery Area

The files in this area can be saved to tape by one of the commands:

- BACKUP RECOVERY AREA
- BACKUP RECOVERY FILES

BACKUP RECOVERY AREA backup on tape all files currently present in the FRA.

The command BACKUP RECOVERY FILES backup on tape all files currently in this area and those who were there but were moved from this area.

☞ **NB:** The FORCE option in the backup clause is ignored e.g the files already saved and identical to the backup will not be saved again.

Monitoring the occupation of the Flash Recovery Area

You should regularly monitor the space occupied in the area to avoid a problem of lack of space. To do this, in addition to the utilization displayed in the home page of Enterprise Manager,

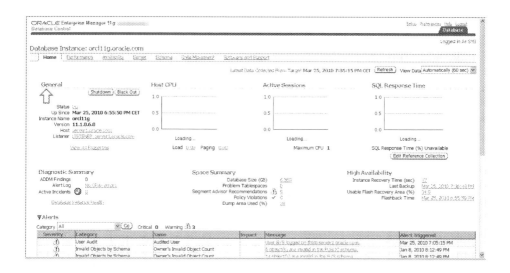

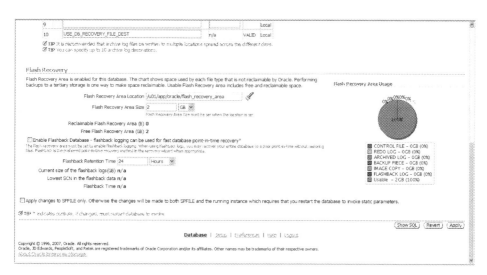

You can query the views V$FLASH_RECOVERY_AREA_USAGE OR V$RECOVERY_FILE_DEST

89

V$RECOVER_FILE_DEST

Name: location of the flash recovery area

Space_limit : size of the flash recovery area

Space_used : size of space used

Space_reclaimable: amount of space that could be recovered after deletion of obsolete items

Number_of_files:number of files in the Flash Recovery Area

V$FLASH_RECOVERY_AREA_USAGE

It contains information similar to the view V$RECOVERY FILE_ DEST but divided by types of files (backup set, archived logs, image copy, control file, flashback log, redo log...).

FILE_TYPE

PERCENT_SPACE_USED

PERCENT_SPACE_RECLAIMABLE

NUMBER_OF_FILES

II—4 BACKUP SUGGESTED BY ORACLE

When performing a Backup using Enterprise Manager, you can choose the strategy suggested by Oracle.

This allows you to make an incremental cumulative backup as backup copies which will be updated incrementally.

The RMAN script launched by this strategy is as follows :

```
run {allocate channel oem_disk_backup device type disk;
recover copy of database with tag 'ORA$OEM_LEVEL_0';
backup incremental level 1 cumulative copies=1 for
recover of copy with tag 'ORA$OEM_LEVEL_0' database;}
```

It works as follows:

At the first launch, the RECOVER command does nothing, no copy of the database have not yet been created;

The Backup command performs a full backup of the database as a copy of images.

In the second launch, the RECOVER command still does nothing, the delta have not yet been created;

Backup command performs cumulative incremental backups (deltas) to a level one that will be used by RECOVER command from the third launch to update the copies of the database created earlier.

RMAN can use the copy images updated for a physical restoration, as it would use a complete image copy, making the process faster.

For the implementation of this strategy, proceed as follows:

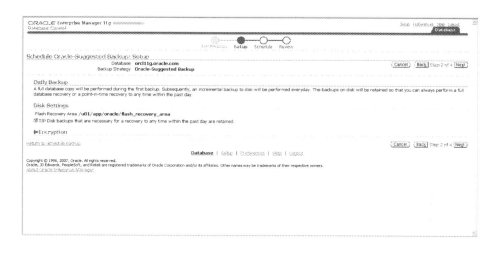

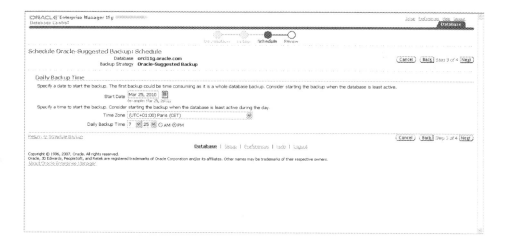

N.B You must specify a date and a frequency

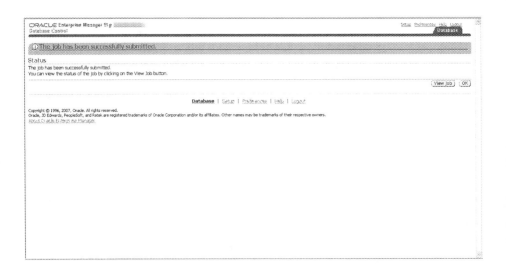

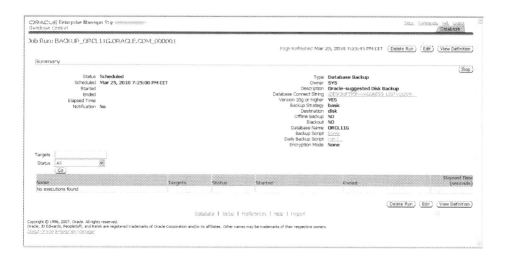

You can follow the progress of the job by pressing the on refresh

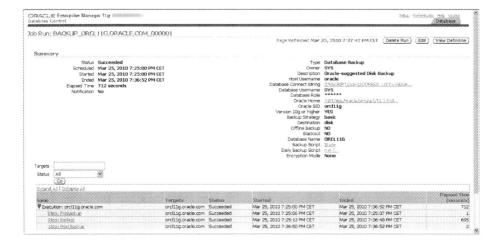

## CHAPTER 3

FLASHBACK TECHNOLOGIES

III-1 FLASHBACK DATABASE

Flashback database is a revolutionary technology introduced in version 10g of Oracle database. It can bring your database to a previous point in time without passing by a restoration followed by a recovery ; which is the case with incomplete recovery.

INCOMPLETE RECOVERY FIGURE

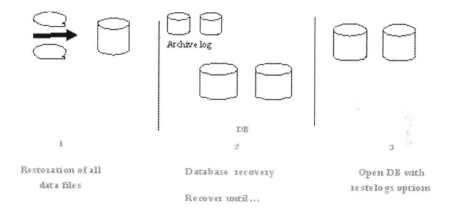

FLASBACK DATABASE FIGURE

Operation Flashback DB

The Flashback Database operation is done using the flashback logs stored in the flash recovery area. When the mode flashback database is enabled, a new process RVWR is launched which will write changes in the database (not all changes unlike the LGWR process) into the buffer located in SGA to flashback logs.

Configuration of flashback database

The configuration is done in four steps:

1) activation of ARCHIVELOG
2) configuration of the flash recovery area
3) definition of the retention period desired
4) activation of the flashback database

The first two steps have already been described above, we will describe below the last two by SQL commands:

- Stop and restart the database in MOUNT Exclusive mode (the option exclusive is required if the database is not single instance, the default mode being MOUNT SHARED)

```
SQL> SHUTDOWN IMMEDIATE;
SQL> STARTUP MOUNT EXCLUSIVE;
```

- Definition of time going back desired by assigning a value (in minutes) to dynamic initialization parameter DB_FLASHBACK_RETENTION_TARGET
```
SQL> ALTER SYSTEM SET DB_FLASHBACK_RETENTION_
TARGET = 1440
```
(as here 24 hours)

- Enable flashback database and opening of the database
```
SQL> ALTER DATABASE FLASHBACK ON;
SQL> ALTER DATABASE OPEN;
```

Configuration by Enterprise Manager

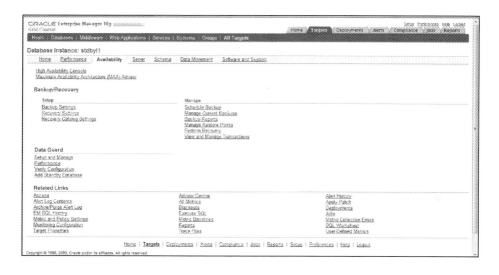

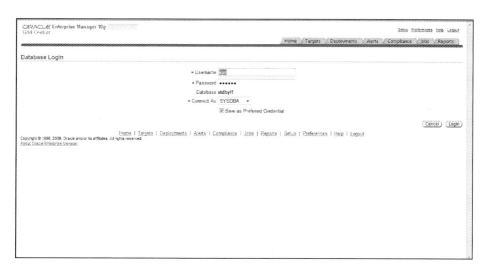

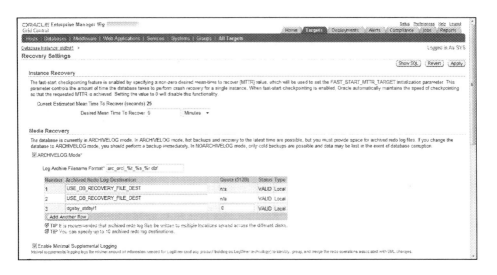

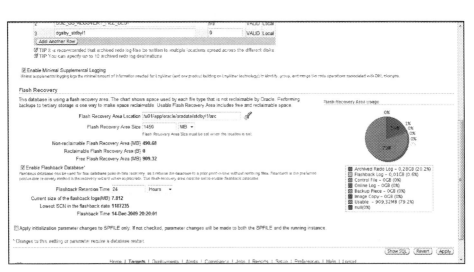

Is the retention period still covered?

No, because the flashback logs stored in the flash recovery area can be automatically overwritten if the space is required in this area for new elements (backups, ARCHIVELOG, new flashback logs . . .) unless you create a guaranteed restore point (see below).
Similarly, flashback logs may be kept beyond the retention period set if there is space in the flash recovery area

Guaranteed Restore Point

This Guaranteed Restore Point stored indefinitely in the control file (unless it is explicitly deleted) will bring the database to a point in time later than or equal to at least the creation of this.
This backward movement is possible even if the flashback database mode has not been activated.
If this mode is activated, flashback logs are preserved to make it back in time, if, of course the space in the area allows this storage.

Syntax for creating a restore point

```
SQL> CREATE RESTORE POINT name_restore_point
[AS OF {TIMESTAMP|SCN} value]
[{PRESERVE | GUARANTIE FLASHBACK DATABASE}]
```

Up to **2048** normal restore points are kept for at least the number of days assigned to the parameter normal CONTROL_FILE_RECORD_ KEEP_TIME. To store them beyond, use the clause PRESERVE.
The clause AS OF lets you create a restore point which takes effect from the past time specified by either TIMESTAMP or SCN value.

☞ **NB:** The clauses AS OF and PRESERVE are only available since 11g version.

Remove by the command
```
SQL> DROP RESTORE POINT name_restore_point;
```

Restore points can be read in the V$RESTORE_POINT view.

```
SQL> SELECT NAME, SCN, TIME, GUARANTEE_FLASHBACK_DATABASE,
RESTORE_POINT_TIME FROM V$RESTORE_POINT_TIME
```

FLASHBACK DATABASE LIMITATIONS

You cannot use flashback database in the following cases:

- The control file was recreated
- A tablespace has been deleted
- Space has been reclaimed in a data file.

Target point T1   one of the three actions below done   **T2 actual point**

From T2 impossible return to T1
In these cases, use the incomplete recovery to return to the time before these actions.

USING FLASBACK DATABASE

FLASHBACK DATABASE command can be done in SQL as well as in RMAN, the database being in exclusive MOUNT mode. As a target point, you can use:

- Time
- SCN
- The sequence number of log
- A restore point.

☞ Examples

RMAN>flashback database To TIME=
TO_DATE ('2009-10-05 19: 00: 00 ', 'YYYY-MM-DD HH24: MI: SS');
RMAN>flashback database to sequence = 200;

SQL>flashback database TO TIMESTAMP sysdate-1;
SQL>flashback database TO SCN 12458;
SQL>flashback database TO RESTORE POINT restore_point_name;
SQL>flashback database TO TIMESTAMP
TO_TIMESTAMP (TO_DATE ('2009-10-09 14: 25: 00',
'YYYY-MM-DD HH24: MISS'));

RMAN>flashback database To before resetlogs;
Allows to bring the database to the state before the last RESETLOGS operation. After the operation flasback database, open the database with RESETLOGS option.
```
SQL> ALTER DATABASE OPEN RESETLOGS;
```

☞ **NB:** It is advisable to open the database in read only mode, then check if the target point has been reached in consulting e.g. column CURRENT_SCN of the V$DATABASE view.

If the return was not as backward as desired, you can immediately repeat the flashback operation before the availability of database to the users. On the other hand, if the return was too far back, you use the command RECOVER UNTIL to advance.

The RECOVER command is the opposite of FLASHBACK DATABASE, even if it takes you back in the past, this is possible because it is made from a restoration of the database made at a time even earlier than the target point where we want to bring the database.

Exclusion of a tablespace from flashback database

If some of your tablespaces don't have a critical importance, they can be excluded from a flashback database operation.

By doing so, flashback log data are not generated when operations (DML or DDL) are performed on objects belonging to these tablespaces. After the flashback operation, you will retrieve these excluded tablespaces by performing a recovery.

Proceed as follows:

1) Ensure that the tablespaces to be excluded have backups;

2) SQL> ALTER TABLESPACE tblsp_name FLASHBACK OFF;
   The column FLASHBACK _ON of the V$TABLESPACE view tells us whether or not the tablespace is excluded;
3) Before starting the operation flashback database, put the excluded tablespace offline
   SQL> ALTER TABLESPACE tblsp_name OFFLINE;
4) Start the operation flashback database;
5) Before opening the database, proceed to the recovery of the tablespace excluded.

Flashback database with a tablespace excluded from the flashback.

After the flashback database operation, if you open the database directly with RESETLOGS option, the tablespace file data being offline, it may be permanently lost. According to the versions of Oracle, you receive a warning or not. Even a restoration and recovery will not bring the tablespaces in its current state.

<u>sample</u>

```
SQL>CREATE TABLESPACE TEST DATAFILE '/u01/app/oracle/
oradata/orcl11g/test0 1.dbf' SIZE 100M;
TABLESPACE CREATED.
```

a) Creation of a copy of table hr. employees in tablespace test
```
SQL> CREATE TABLE HR.EMP_TEST TABLESPACE TEST AS
SELECT * FROM HR.EMPLOYEES;
TABLE CREATED.
```

b) Excluding tablespace test from flashback
```
SQL> ALTER TABLESPACE TEST FLASHBACK OFF;
Tablespace altered.
```

c) Note the current_SCN and total amount for salary in table hr. employees
```
SQL> select current_scn from v$database;
CURRENT_SCN
----------------------------------
```

```
42297372
SQL> select sum (salary) from hr.employees;
select sum(salary) from hr.employees;
SUM(SALARY)
---------------
691400
```

d) Multiply the salary colum by 10 for each line of the two tables, validate and note the new current_scn

```
SQL>update hr.employees set salary = salary * 10;
SQL>107 rows updated.
SQL>commit;
Commit complete.
SQL> select sum (salary) from hr.employees;
SQL>SUM (SALARY)
---------------
6914000
SQL> update hr.emp_test set salary=salary * 10;
107 rows update
SQL> commit;
Commit complete.
SQL> select current_scn from v$database;
CURRENT_SCN
-----------
42298900
```

e) Set the tablespace test offline

```
SQL> ALTER TABLESPACE TEST OFFLINE;
```

f) Flashback database and tablespace test recovery.

```
SQL>shutdown immediate;
SQL>exit;
[oracle@server1 ~]$ rman target /
Recovery Manager: Release 11.1.0.6.0—Production
on Thu Mar 25 22:09:55 2010
Copyright (c) 1982, 2007, Oracle. All rights
reserved.
```

```
Connected to target database: ORCL11G
(DBID=813600581, not open)
RMAN> startup mount

Oracle instance started
database mounted

Total System Global Area 314572800 bytes

Fixed Size 1261516 bytes
Variable Size 255852596 bytes
Database Buffers 50331648 bytes
Redo Buffers 7127040 bytes

RMAN> sql 'alter database datafile 7 offline';

using target database control file instead of
recovery catalog
sql statement: alter database datafile 7 offline

RMAN> flashback database to scn 42297372;

Starting flashback at 25-MAR-10
allocated channel: ORA_DISK_1
channel ORA_DISK_1: sid=157 devtype=DISK
starting media recovery
media recovery failed
RMAN-00571:
======================================================
RMAN-00569: ======== ERROR MESSAGE STACK FOLLOWS
==============
RMAN-00571:
======================================================
RMAN-03002: failure of flashback command at
10/29/2010 13:25:00
ORA-38795: warning: FLASHBACK succeeded but
OPEN RESETLOGS would get error belowORA-01245:
offline file 7 will be lost if RESETLOGS is done
```

```
ORA-01110: data file 7: '/u01/app/oracle/
oradata/orcl11g/test01.dbf'
```

Flashback failed because the for drop clause has not been used; add it and issue the command again.

```
RMAN> sql 'alter database datafile 7 offline for
drop';
sql statement: alter database datafile 7 offline
for drop

RMAN> flashback database to scn 42297372;
Starting flashback at 25-MAR-10
using channel ORA_DISK_1
starting media recovery
media recovery complete, elapsed time: 00:00:07
Finished flashback at 25-MAR-10

RMAN> alter database open resetlogs;
database opened
```

RMAN> restore datafile 7;
Starting restore at 25-MAR-10
Using target database control file instead of recovery catalog
Allocated channel: ORA_DISK_1
Channel ORA_DISK_1: SID=152 device type=DISK
Channel ORA_DISK_1: restoring datafile 00007
Input datafile copy RECID=6 STAMP=714598553 file name=/ u01/app/oracle/flash_reco very_area/ORCL11G/datafile/o1_mf_ test_5tqc81sz_.dbf
Destination for restore of datafile 00007: /u01/app/oracle/oradata/ orcl11g/test0 1.dbf
Channel ORA_DISK_1: copied datafile copy of datafile 00007
Output file name=/u01/app/oracle/oradata/orcl11g/test01.dbf RECID=0 STAMP=0
Finished restore at 25-MAR-10
RMAN> recover datafile 7;
Starting recover at 25-MAR-10

Using channel ORA_DISK_1
Starting media recovery
Media recovery complete, elapsed time: 00:00:00
Finished recover at 25-MAR-10
RMAN> SQL 'alter database datafile 7 online';
SQL statement: alter database datafile 7 online
SQL> alter tablespace test online;
Tablespace altered.
h)   Check the total amount salary for the table hr.emp_test and hr.employees
SQL> select sum (salary) from hr.emp_test;
SUM (SALARY)

691400
SQL> select sum (salary) from hr.employees;
SUM (SALARY)

691400

The content of the table emp_test has been reverted to its state at SCN used for the flashback database operation.
The Recover command cannot bring the table emp_test at its content after multiplication the salary by 10 although we perform a recovery without UNTIL clause. This is normal because a new incarnation of the database has been done before, and Recovery cannot be extended through various incarnations of the database.

Monitoring Flashback Database.

- The V$FLASHBACK _DATABASE_LOG view permits to obtain information on:

  - The SCN and the time to which the database can be brought back.
  - Size in bytes occupied by the flashback log and the estimated size to meet the retention period.

```
SQL> SELECT ESTIMATED_FLASHBACK_SIZE, FLASHBACK_
SIZE, OLDEST_FLASHBACK_SCN, OLDEST_FLASHBACK_TIME
FROM V$FLASHBACK_DATABASE_LOG;
```

- The V$FLASHBACK _DATABASE_STAT view contains the overhead of logging flashback data in the flashback database logs. It contains the last 24 hours of information, each line corresponding to an interval of one hour.

```
V$FLASHBACK_DATABASE_STAT
Begin_time : start time
End_time : End Time
Flashback_data : size of flashback logs generated
during the period
db_data : size of data generated during the period
Redo_data: size of redo log data generated during
the period
Estimated_flashback_data: Estimated size of flashback
logs during the period
(sizes are in bytes).
```

III-2 OTHER FLASHBACK TECHNOLOGIES

There exist other flashback technologies which we will develop, some permitting to make a "repair" after an erroneous operation.

TECHNOLOGIES	USED FOR	WORKS WITH	MADE ONLINE
FLASHBACK TO BEFORE DROP	RESTORE A DROPPED TABLE	RECYCLE BIN	YES
FLASHBACK TABLE	CANCELL WRONG CHANGES (BY DML)	UNDO DATA	YES
FLASHBACK QUERY	SEE THE VALUES OF DATA MODIFIED BY A TRANSACTION	UNDO DATA	YES
FLASHBACK VERSION QUERY	TEMPORAL NAVIGATION	UNDO DATA	YES
TRANSACTION QUERY	RESEARCH AND CANCELLATION OF TRANSACTION	UNDO DATA	YES
DATA ARCHIVE	PRESERVATION OF HISTORICAL DATA	TABLESPACE CONTAINING FLASHBACK DATA	YES
FLASHBACK DATABASE	CANCEL THE WRONG UPDATES (DML, DROP TRUN CATE)	FLASHBAK LOG	NO
TRANSACTION BACKOUT	REVERT ON TRANSACTION	UNDO DATA	YES

FLASHBACK DROP

Since version 10g, a table deleted by DROP TABLE statement is sent in the recycle bin and can be retrieved by the instruction [FLASHBACK TABLE TO BEFORE DROP] as it is not withdrawn. For the table (and some related objects) to be put in the trash, the dynamic session initialization parameter RECYCLEBIN must be at ON (default value) The recycle bin is located in the tablespace containing the table. Deleted objects are not moved but renamed. They appear in the views XXX_ TABLES, XXX_SEGMENTS, XXX_ objects, XXX_recyclebin with a new name beginning with BIN, XXX ∈ {USER, ALL, DBA}. Column Dropped of view XXX_ TABLES indicates whether or not the table is in the recycle bin.

☞ **N.B:**
These objects appear in the view XXX_OBJETCS, XXX_TABLES only for Oracle 10gR1 versions. On the other hand they appear in XXX_segments in all versions after 10g (10gR1 to 11g R2)

☞ **Example:**
Drop the table employees which has a primary key PK_employees.
```
SQL> DROP TABLE HR.EMPLOYEES;
SQL> select * from V$version;
BANNER
--------------------------------------------------

Oracle Database 11g Enterprise Edition Release
11.1.0.6.0—Production
PL / SQL Release 11.1.0.6.0—Production
CORE 11.1.0.6.0 Production
TNS for Linux:Version 11.1.0.6.0—Production
NLSRTL Version 11.1.0.6.0—Production

SQL> select owner, segment_name, segment_type from dba_
segments WHERE segment_name like 'BIN%';
```

OWNER	SEGMENT_ NAME	SEGMENT_ TYPE
HR	BIN$gxuZDSd0urPgQAB/AQBuFg= = $0	TABLE
HR	BIN$gxuZDSdsurPgQAB/AQBuFg= = $0	INDEX
HR	BIN$gxuZDSdturPgQAB/AQBuFg= = $0	INDEX
HR	BIN$gxuZDSduurPgQAB/AQBuFg= = $0	INDEX
HR	BIN$gxuZDSdvurPgQAB/AQBuFg= = $0	INDEX
HR	BIN$gxuZDSdwurPgQAB/AQBuFg= = $0	INDEX
HR	BIN$gxuZDSdxurPgQAB/AQBuFg= = $0	INDEX

7 rows selected.

```
SQL> select object_name from dba_objects WHERE
object_name like 'BIN$%';
```

No rows selected

```
SQL> select table_name from dba_tables where
dropped<>'NO';
No rows selected
```

While the table is in the trash, it can be recovered by:
```
SQL> FLASHBACK TABLE HR.EMPLOYEES TO BEFORE DROP
[RENAME TO newname];
```

Where several tables are in the recycle bin with the same original name, Flashback works on the mechanism LIFO (LAST IN, FIRST OUT). The last recently dropped table will be retrieved. If you want to bring a specific table, you must specify the new name assigned after removal that you can get consulting DBA_ RECYCLEBIN (column OBJECT_NAME)

RECOVERY OF SPACE IN THE TRASH
Auto Recovery

The objects in the trash can be automatically withdrawn if the Oracle server needs the space for new created objects. The order of allocation of extensions is the following:

- The free extents in the tablespace are used
- Extents used by deleted items are used
- Tablespace is extended if the clause autoextend is ON

Prior to recovery, you can query the DBA_RECYCLEBIN view.

```
DBA_RECYCLEBIN
OBJET_NAME: NAME IN THE TRASH
ORIGINAL_NAME: NAME OF THE OBJECT BEFORE REMOVAL
RELATED: NUMBER OF THE OBJECT
DROPTIME: TIME OF REMOVAL
CAN_UNDROP: Object can be restored (YES) OR (NO).
SPACE: OCCUPIED SPACE IN BYTES
```

▶ **Remark:**

The indexes of tables deleted after the flashback operation don't have their original names. So remember to rename them if these names are required by some applications.

Manual recovery

The command Sql PURGE can permanently delete items in the trash.

Simplified Syntax

```
SQL> PURGE {[TABLE table_name |INDEX index_name]};
SQL> PURGE TABLESPACE tblsp_name [USER user_name];
SQL> PURGE {USER_RECYCLEBIN |DBA_RECYCLEBIN} ;
```

To force the permanent removal of the table, add the clause PURGE to the command DROP.

```
SQL> DROP TABLE tablename PURGE;
```

RESTRICTIONS ON A FLASHBACK DROP

You cannot use FLASHBACK DROP in the tables below:

- Reside in the tablespace SYSTEM
- Reside in a tablespace managed through the data dictionary
- Using Fine Grained Audit or Virtual Private Database srategies

Similarly, during a FLASHBACK DROP items below are not brought back:

- Referential integrity constraints
- Bitmap join indexes
- log materialized views
- indexes deleted before the tables

EXERCISE

- Under the system, check that the bin is activated
- Display the names of constraints and their types of the table hr. employees
- Display the index of the table for employees
- Count the number of items after deletion
- Check for user_recyclebin to display the columns object_name, original_name, drop time, can_undrop

Comment

- Count the number of employees
- Recover the dropped table from the trash
- Count back the number of employees and make sure that the user_recyclebin is empty
- Display the names of table indexes used.
- Display the referential integrity constraints, what do you notice?

```
SQL> conn / as sysdba
Connected.
SQL> show parameter recyclebin
NAME              TYPE            VALUE
-----------------------------------
recyclebin        string          on
SQL> conn hr/hr.
Connected
SQL> select constraint_name,constraint_type from
user_CONSTRAINTS
2 > where table_name='EMPLOYEES';

CONSTRAINT_NAME                       C
----------------
EMP_LAST_NAME_NN                      C
EMP_EMAIL_NN                          C
EMP_HIRE_DATE_NN                      C
EMP_JOB_NN                            C
EMP_SALARY_MIN                        C
EMP_EMAIL_UK                          U
EMP_EMP_ID_PK                         P
EMP_MANAGER_FK                        R
EMP_JOB_FK                            R
EMP_DEPT_FK                           R
10 rows selected.
SQL> select index_name from user_indexes where
table_name='EMPLOYEES';
INDEX_NAME
--------------------------
EMP_NAME_IX
EMP_MANAGER_IX
EMP_JOB_IX
EMP_DEPARTMENT_IX
EMP_EMP_ID_PK
EMP_EMAIL_UK
6 rows selected.
SQL> select count (*) from user_objects;
```

```
  COUNT (*)
------------
      35
SQL> drop table employees cascade constraints; Table
dropped.
SQL> select count (*) from user_objects;
  COUNT (*)
------------
      26
SQL> select object_name,original_name,droptime,can_
undrop from user_recyclebin;
OBJECT_NAME        ORIGINAL_NAME     DROPTIME    CAN
----------------------------------------------------
BIN$gspCWalxzuDgQAB/AQBS7A==$0 EMP_DEPARTMENT_IX
2010-03-27:15:40:20 NO
BIN$gspCWalyzuDgQAB/AQBS7A==$0 EMP_JOB_IX
2010-03-27:15:40:20 NO
BIN$gspCWalzzuDgQAB/AQBS7A==$0 EMP_MANAGER_IX
2010-03-27:15:40:20 NO
BIN$gspCWal0zuDgQAB/AQBS7A==$0 EMP_NAME_IX
2010-03-27:15:40:20 NO

BIN$gspCWal1zuDgQAB/AQBS7A==$0 EMP_EMAIL_UK
2010-03-27:15:40:20 NO
BIN$gspCWal2zuDgQAB/AQBS7A==$0 EMP_EMP_ID_PK
2010-03-27:15:40:20 NO
BIN$gspCWal3zuDgQAB/AQBS7A==$0 SECURE_EMPLOYEES
2010-03-27:15:40:20 NO
BIN$gspCWal4zuDgQAB/AQBS7A==$0 UPDATE_JOB_HISTORY
2010-03-27:15:40:20 NO
BIN$gspCWal5zuDgQAB/AQBS7A==$0 EMPLOYEES
2010-03-27:15:40:20 YES
9 rows selected.
SQL> select count (*) from employees; select count
(*) from employees *
ERROR at line 1:
ORA-00942: table or view does not exist
SQL> flashback table employees to before drop ;
```

```
Flashback complete.
SQL> select count (*) from employees;
  COUNT (*)
-------------
      107
SQL> select
object_name,original_name,droptime,can_undrop from
user_recyclebin;
no rows selected
SQL> select index_name from user_indexes where
table_name='EMPLOYEES';

INDEX_NAME
-------------------------------
BIN$gspCWal0zuDgQAB/AQBS7A==$0
BIN$gspCWalzzuDgQAB/AQBS7A==$0
BIN$gspCWalyzuDgQAB/AQBS7A==$0
BIN$gspCWalxzuDgQAB/AQBS7A==$0
BIN$gspCWal2zuDgQAB/AQBS7A==$0
BIN$gspCWal1zuDgQAB/AQBS7A==$0
6 rows selected.
```

THE INDEX ARE RECOVERED BUT NOT WITH THEIR NAMES OF ORIGIN

```
SQL> select constraint_name,constraint_type from
user_CONSTRAINTS where table_name='EMPLOYEES' and
constraint_type='R';
no rows selected
```

THE referential integrity constraints are LOST

FLASHBACK TABLE

Flashback table allows to bring back the contents of a table at a time earlier than the committed changes made on it

Flashback Table

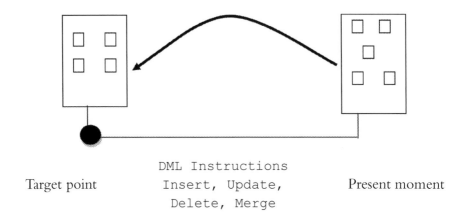

Target point   DML Instructions   Present moment
                  Insert, Update,
                  Delete, Merge

The operation is done on site (the table is readable) and an exclusive lock is placed on it. It works by using undo data.

```
SQL> flashback Table hr.employees TO SCN 1434;
SQL> flashback Table hr.employees TO TIMESTAMP
TO_TIMESTAMP
('2009-10-09 12:45:00', 'YYYY-MM-DD HH24:MI:SS');
```

☞ **NB:** You must first have enabled row movement in the table by the command
SQL> ALTER TABLE HR.EMPLOYEES ENABLE ROW MOVEMENT ;

You can check the column ROW_MOVEMENT of the DBA_TABLES view to see whether the row movement is allowed.

RESTRICTIONS ON A FLASHBACK TABLE

- Flashback table cannot be applied to tables owned by SYS or to remote tables

- Flashback Table cannot go back to a point in time prior to the execution of a DDL that has changed the structure of the table or recovered space (ALTER TABLE SHRINK SPACE), on the other hand this restriction does not apply to DDL changing only the storage attributes of the table.

FLASHBACK DATA ARCHIVE

Flashback table and different versions of flashback query work with undo data. The retention period of these data is limited by the parameter UNDO_RETENTION and space availiable in UNDO tablespace. These technologies are therefore not suitable if you want to find the changes over a long period. (Some organizations are obliged by law to trace the history of changes over a period of up to ten years).

The new feature FLASHBACK DATA ARCHIVE(also called TOTAL RECALL) introduced in 11 g is appropriate in this case.
It allows storing any changes to your data as long as you want. Once the retention period is reached, the oldest data are automatically deleted.

Implementation of flashback data archive

- Grant the privilege FLASHBACK ARCHIVE ADMINISTER to users so they can execute instructions {create | alter | drop} flashback archive.
  ```
  SQL> GRANT FLASHBACK ARCHIVE ADMINISTER TO userx;
  ```

- Create flashback data archive
  ```
  SQL> CREATE FLASHBACK DATA ARCHIVE flash1
  TABLESPACE flash_tbs1 RETENTION 2 year [quota
  size];
  ```

- The absence of a quota means that the archive data can occupy all the space in the tablespace.

Here, Data archives will be kept for two years and automatically purged beyond these two years.

- Allow access to a flashback data archive to a user
  ```
  SQL> GRANT FLASHBACK ARCHIVE ON flash1 TO
  userx;
  ```

- Grant the EXECUTE privilege on the package DBMS_
  FLASHBACK_ARCHIVE (This step is optional, required if
  you want users to run this package)
  ```
  SQL> GRANT EXECUTE ON DBMS_FLASHBACK_ARCHIVE
  TO userx;
  ```

- You can also change the flashback either for example to change
  the quota, purge or manually specify a flashback archive default
  for the system, add or delete a tablespace, change the retention
  period.

  ```
  SQL> ALTER FLASHBACK ARCHIVE FLASH1 SET
  DEFAULT;
  SQL>ALTER FLASHBACK ARCHIVE FLASH1 MODIFY
  TABLESPACE flash_tblsp1 QUOTA 5G;

  SQL> ALTER FLASHBACK ARCHIVE FLASH1 PURGE
  BEFORE TIMESTAMP
  (SYSTIMESTAMP-INTERVAL '2' MONTH);
  TO CLEAR THE ARCHIVES OLD OF MORE THAN 2
  MONTHS.
  SQL> ALTER FLASHBACK ARCHIVE flash1 ADD
  TABLESPACE flash_tbsp;
  SQL> ALTER FLASHBACK ARCHIVE flash1 REMOVE
  TABLESPACE
  flash_tbslp1;
  SQL> ALTER FLASHBACK flash1 MODIFY RETENTION
  4 YEAR;
  ```

Enable/Disable FLASHBACK DATA ARCHIVE.

Once the flashback data archive created and privileges granted, authorized users can activate the storage of archival data during the creation of the table or after it by the command alter specifying the clause ARCHIVE

```
SQL> CREATE TABLE test_archive (...) FLASHBACK
ARCHIVE [flash1];
SQL> ALTER TABLE test_archive (...) FLASHBACK
ARCHIVE [flash2] ;
```
If no flashback data archive is specified, the default flashback (if any) will be used

```
SQL> alter table test_archive no flashback archive;
```
Ends the recording of data archives.

Once flashback data archive activated, any DML order (except insert) will cause the record in the archive flashback
These archival data can't be updated unless the disassociation is made between the table and the flashback data archive (see below).

Example of consulting historical data

```
SQL> SELECT versions_xid last_name, salary FROM
employees versions BETWEEN TIMESTAMP t1 and t2 where
EMPLOYEE_ID=200;
```

Restrictions

If flashback data archive is active on a table, the following operations on the latter are prohibited in 11gR1 :

-   Deletion, modification, renaming columns
-   Converting a LONG column to LOB
-   Issuing DROP TABLE or TRUNCATE TABLE on this table
-   Partitioning the table

In 11gR2 version, only DROP TABLE and complex DDL such as partitioning are prohibited. Nevertheless, the execution of the procedure DBMS_FLASHBACK_ARCHIVE.DISASSOCIATE (OWNER, TABLE_NAME) temporarily dissociates the given table from the flashback data archive and allows you to run the instructions below. To reassociate the table with the flashback data archive, run DBMS_FLASHBACK_ARCHIVE.REASSOCIATE (OWNER, TABLE_NAME)

Monitoring flashback data archive

The following views permits to monitor Flashback database
DBA_FLASHBACK_ARCHIVE_TABLES : DETAILS ON THE TABLES for which Flashback Data Archive is enabled.

DBA_FLASHBACK_ARCHIVE : CONTAINS ALL THE FLASHBACK DATA ARCHIVE PRESENT IN THE DATABASE. The STATUS column of this view indicates whether the flashback archive is the default flashback archive for the database (DEFAULT) or not (NULL).

DBA_FLASHBACK_ARCHIVE_TS: contains details about tablespaces storing FLASH_BACK_DATA_ARCHIVE (name of tablespaces and their quota)

TRANSACTION BACKOUT

With Flashback Transaction query and flashback query of Oracle Database 10g version, you can correct logical errors by looking first, past data and then applying UNDO_SQL instruction to revert the instructions one by one.

With the new technology, FLASHBACK TRANSACTION BACKOUT introduced in 11g version, you can undo changes made by a transaction as well as dependent transactions using a single instruction (the DBMS_FLASHBACK.TRANSACTION_BACKOUT procedure).

A transaction can have either a dependent write_after_write relationship, or a relationship of primary key constraint, or a foreign key dependency.

- In a write_after_write relationship, the dependent transaction alters the data that was previously amended by the parent transaction.
- In a primary key relationship, the dependent transaction reinserts the primary key deleted by the parent transaction.
- Foreign key dependency
  In table b, column b1 has a foreign key constraint on colum a1 of table a. T1 changes a value in a1, and later transaction T2 changes a value in b1.

Transaction backout configuration

First, ensure that the database is in ARCHIVELOG mode and:

- Enable supplemental logging
  SQL> ALTER DATABASE ADD SUPPLEMENTAL LOG DATA;
  SQL> ALTER DATABASE ADD SUPPLEMENTAL LOG DATA
  (PRIMARY KEY) COLUMNS;
- Grant the EXECUTE privilege on the package DBMS_
  FLASHBACK to desired users
  SQL> GRANT EXECUTE ON DBMS_FLASHBACK TO userx;
- Grant the CREATE ANY TABLE privilege to users desired.
  SQL> GRANT CREATE ANY TABLE TO userx;
- Grant the SELECT ANY TRANSACTION privilege to users desired.
  SQL> GRANT SELECT ANY TRANSACTION TO userx;

To undo changes made by a transaction.

SQL> EXECUTE DBMS_FLASHBACK.TRANSACTION_BACKOUT

(NUMTXNS	⇨	Number of Transactions passed as input,
Xids	⇨	Transaction list number in an array form,
Options	⇨	dbms_flashback.nocascade)

Options can be :

NOCASCADE: when the transaction does not have a dependent transaction (default value)

CASCADE: cancel the dependent transaction before the parent transaction

NOCASCADE_FORCE: cancel only the parent transaction, dependent transactions are ignored.

NOCONFLICT_ONLY: only the lines of the parent transaction which do not generate conflict are canceled.

Monitoring

After executing the TRANSACTION_BACKOUT, the views DBA_FLASHBACK_TXN_STATE and DBA_FLASHBACK_TXN_ REPORT are populated.

DBA_FLASHBACK_TXN_STATE
Xid
Dependent _ xid
Backout_mode
Username: user who ran the cancellation

The view DBA_FLASHBACK_TXN _REPORT contains more details on the transaction canceled (column XID_REPORT in XML format).

## CHAPTER 4

DUPLICATING A DATABASE &
TABLESPACE POINT IN TIME RECOVERY

II-1 DUPLICATE A DATABASE WITH RMAN

For testing purposes, you may be asked to work on a copy of your database production. In this case, you'll duplicate your target database, this method is also used to create a standby database (see the second part of this book)

PREREQUISITES

- The same version of OS must be on the source and target
- The same version of Oracle software must be installed on both systems (the release may differ)

Steps to follow to clone a database

- Create a password file for auxiliary instance (the one that will host the duplicated database)
- From the target instance (the one that contains the database to be duplicated) establish a connection to auxiliary instance. The connection to the target is not mandatory if either you are connected to a recovery catalog and the auxiliary instance has access to the RMAN backup or you are just connected to the auxiliary which must have access to a disk BACKUP LOCATION (11g only).
- Create an initialization parameters file for the auxiliary instance.
- Start the Auxiliary Instance in NOMOUNT mode.
- Start the target instance in MOUNT mode at the minimum.
- Check the availability of backups and archived logs.

▶ **Caution:**

DUPLICATE command will fail if the backups are not copied manually on the server hosting the auxiliary instance and this in respect of the initial paths on the target. If you are using 11g version, you can run duplication with FROM ACTIVE DATABASE option, in this case the copy of backups is no longer necessary.

- Allocation of additional channels to speed up the copy (optional)
- Execute the command DUPLICATE.

1) Creation of the password file.

$orapwd file = $ORACLE_HOME /dbs /orapw <SID> password = oracle.

→ It is recommended to assign the same password as that assigned to the target database.

2) Establishment of connectivity.

You can use netmgr (See details in section 7 on page 172)

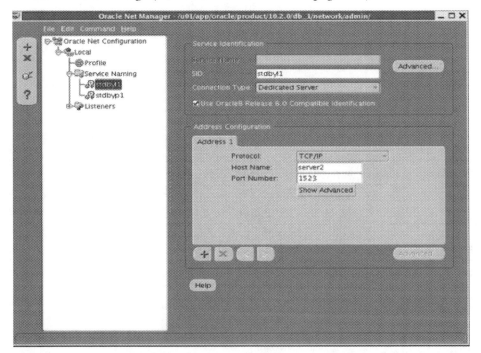

3) Creation of the initialization parameter file for auxiliary instance.

This file must contain at least the following parameters:

- DB_NAME: name of the duplicated database
- DB_BLOCK_SIZE: must be identical to that of the target database
- CONTROL_FILES: Location of control files
- DB_FILE_NAME_CONVERT and LOG_FILE_NAME_ CONVERT respectively indicate the substitution of the location of data files and redo logfiles from the target. Contains even values. Recommended even though not required if the files are duplicated on the same location as the target files.

Example:

```
DB_FILE_NAME_CONVERT      ='/u01/app/oracle/oradata/
orcl', '/u01/app/oracle/oradata/aux'
```

In place of these two parameters, you can use LOGFILE clauses in the DUPLICATE command, or before starting Duplicate, use SET Newname FOR Datafile x TO . . . . in a RUN block, or CONFIGURE

4) Start the Auxiliary Instance

$export ORACLE_SID = aux
$sqlplus / as SYSDBA

SQL>Create Spfile FROM pfile = $HOME/init aux.ora' ;
SQL>Startup NOMOUNT ;

5) Copy the backups and archive on the auxiliary host.

If in V11 you can skip this step (see below)

6) Run the DUPLICATE command on the target host

$export ORACLE_SID=orcl
$rman target / auxiliary sys/oracle@aux

RMAN>RUN {
ALLOCATE Auxiliary Channel aux1

```
DEVICE Type DISK;
SET NEWNAME FOR DATAFILE 3 TO '/u01/app/oracle/
oracle/aux/examples/dbf';
—
DUPLICATE TARGET Database To 'Aux_name';}
```
You can just be connected to the Auxiliary instance, in this case you must issue DUPLICATE DATABASE 'Source_name' TO 'Aux_name' BACKUP LOCATION 'path_name'.

Aux_name be the same assigned to the parameter db_name of the file initialization of the auxiliary instance.

The options commonly used with the DUPLICATE command are:

- NOFILENAMECHECK: Prevents the check of files. Required if the files have the same names and locations on the target and the server hosting the database duplicated.
- SKIP Tablespace: To exclude tablespaces, when duplicating
- SKIP Readonly: Exclude read-only tablespace.
- Until Clause: Recovery Clause
- LOGFILE: Specifies the location of redo logfiles.

To create a standby database

RMAN>DUPLICATE TARGET DATABASE FOR STANDBY;

 Caution:

At the end of the duplication, a new identifier DBID is assigned to the new database unless the database is a standby database. In this case, it retains the same DBID as the source database.

Case for a database 11g version

In 11g version, you can duplicate without first having to make a backup of the database and the copy on the host that will contain the replicated database. This duplication method is called active Duplication or Duplication based network saves CPU time and disk space. RMAN will perform an incomplete recovery when this method is used because the redo logfiles online are not copied. For minimal loss of data, it is recommended that a switch logfile be done before starting the replication. The prerequisites seen above must be completed before issuing the command DUPLICATE.

Simplified syntax

RMAN> DUPLICATE TARGET DATABASE TO dupdb FROM ACTIVE DATABASE
db_file_name_convert 'Old', 'New'
SPFILE
parameter_value_convert 'Old', 'New'
SET log_file_name_convert 'Old', 'New'
Set parameter1_init value1
Set parametern_init valuen

[PASSWORD FILE];
Parameter_value_convert: converts all parameters in SPFile excluding db_file_name_convert and log_file_name_convert. Can be used for example to change the parameter values x_dump_dest

The clause password file allows the use of the target password file to replace the one of the auxiliary.
If the target database is in OPEN state, it must be in ARCHIVELOG MODE

IV-2 TABLESPACE POINT IN TIME RECOVERY (TSPITR)

In case of unwanted committed changes, errors or data corruption whose scope is limited to one or more tablespaces, you can perform TABLESPACE POINT IN TIME RECOVERY without affecting other tablespaces contents. This type of incomplete recovery is called TABLESPACE POINT IN TIME RECOVERY (TSPITR)

During this operation, RMAN performs the following tasks:

1) It restores to an auxiliary instance a backup control file prior to the specified target point.
2) It restores the data files of tablespaces to be recovered including those of tablespaces SYSTEM and UNDO
3) It recovers data files restored up to the target destination.
4) It exports to the target database the given metadata of the data dictionary concerning the objects of the tablespaces recovered.
5) It performs a name change in the control file (by the command SWITCH) so that the recovered data files points to those in the auxiliary instance.
6) It imports the metadata of the data dictionary from the auxiliary instance to the target instance.
7) It deletes all files in the auxiliary instance

Before starting the operation TSPITR

Before executing the TSPITR operation, you must ensure the followings:

1 -Well determine the target point
You can get this using the different options of Flashback (query, flashback data archive) or by viewing the audit trail if auditing has been activated. This target is very important because when using an inappropriate item, you cannot do another operation on the same TSPITR tablespace, unless you use a recovery catalog.

2 -Identify the tablespaces to be recovered
you must determine if the tablespaces to be recovered, is 'self content' or if it contains objects located in another tablespace. For that, you check the TS_PITR_CHECK view. If the tablespace is not 'sef-content' you can:

- Either recover in addition of the tablespace, the tablespaces related
- Remove or suspend the connection between these tablespaces

Example: Recovering tablespace USERS

```
SQL> SELECT OBJ1_NAME, OBJ1_TPYPE, TS1_NAME,
```

```
Obj2_name,   obj2_type,   TS2_name,   Constraint_
name, reason
FOM TS_PITR_CHECK WHERE
(TS1_NAME = 'USERS' AND TS2_NAME <> 'USERS') OR
(TS1_NAME <>'USERS' AND TS2_NAME = 'USERS');
```

3   -Identify the objects that will be lost.
The objects created after the target point will be lost after the operation TSPITR. You should query the view TS_PITR_OBJECTS_TO_BE_DROPPED before the operation, save them by EXPORT for example and import them after the operation by IMPORT.

Different TSPITR modes.

TSPITR may be executed in three ways:

Fully automated:
In this mode, which exists since version 10g, you only need to specify an auxiliary destination, RMAN takes care of everything else. Oracle recommends this method.

Semi-automatic mode:
Unlike the first mode, you can customize the location of your files and the allocation of auxiliary channels.

Manual mode:
In this mode, you configure your auxilliary instance as to duplicate the database.

```
Example of TSPITR with automated mode
$ export ORACLE_SID=ORCL
$rman target /
RMAN> RECOVER TABLESPACE USERS UNTIL SCN 434521
AUXILIARY
DESTINATION '/ u01/app/oracle/oradata/aux';
```

- After the operation TSPITR, the tablespace is offline, save and put it online at the end of the operation.

Caution

If the target point is prior to the time the UNDO TABLESPACE has been changed and is different from the current UNDO tablespace, the following command will fail if you do not have a recovery catalog, unless you add the command UNDO TABLESPACE tblsp_name_undo of the target point.

ACCOUNTS RELATED TO TSPITR

- At the end of TSPIR, the tablespace recovered is offline
- Old recovered tablespace backups are no longer usable, redo a new backup immediately after the operation
- You can perform TSPITR only once on a tablespace, unless you use a recovery catalog.
- You can't perform TSPITR in the following cases:
  - Deleting a tablespace
  - Tablespace renamed and you try to recover it up to a time before the change of name

Impossible recovery

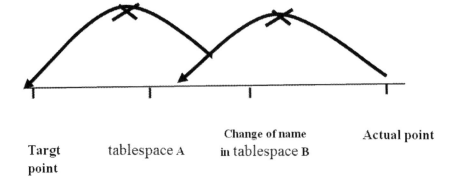

| Targt
point | tablespace A | Change of name
in tablespace B | Actual point |

Comparison between TSPITR Flashback and Incomplete Recovery

We present in the table below situations where unwanted orders were made and the appropriate recovery operations.

OPERATIONS PERFORMED	POSSIBLE RECOVERY OPERATIONS	SUITABLE RECOVERY OPERATION	Prohibited OPERATIONS
DROP TABLE	Flashback DROP, TSPITR, Incomplete Recovery, Flashback Database	Flashback DROP	
TRUNCATE TABLE	TSPITR, Incomplete Recovery, Flashback Database	TSPITR	Flashback DROP
COMMITED DML	Flashback Table, TSPITR, Flashback Database	Flashback Table	
LOGICAL CORRUPTIONS	Flashback Table, TSPITR, Flashback Database	Flashback Table	
DROP TABLESPACE	Incomplete Recovery	Incomplete Recovery	Flashback Database, TSPITR

SECOND PART
DATA GUARD

## CHAPTER 5

INTRODUCTION TO DATA GUARD

V-1 PRESENTATION

Protecting your data by using only the traditional backups have some of the following drawbacks:

> ➤ The recovery time can be long and causing prolonged unavailability of your system.
> ➤ In case of serious disaster (fire, flood, . . .), data and their backups if kept in the same site may be lost.

To address this, ORACLE CORPORATION offers DATA GUARD, the efficient solution of protection against disaster.

ORACLE DATA GUARD is a software infrastructure for managing, monitoring and automation that works with a production database (or primary base) and multiple standby databases to protect data against failures, errors that may destroy your base. It is integrated in Database Enterprise Editions (does not require additional license). Data protection is ensured by features that automate the creation, management and monitoring of databases and other components of a DATA GUARD configuration. DATA GUARD automates the process of maintaining a copy (called a standby database) of the production database. This copy is used when the database is damaged or should be placed offline for any service. From a copy of the master database, you can create up to 9 standby databases (30, if in 11gR2 version). Since version 10g, standby database can be cascaded (a standby database can have 9 (30 in version 11gR2) standby databases. The combination of the primary database and its standby databases is a DATA GUARD configuration.

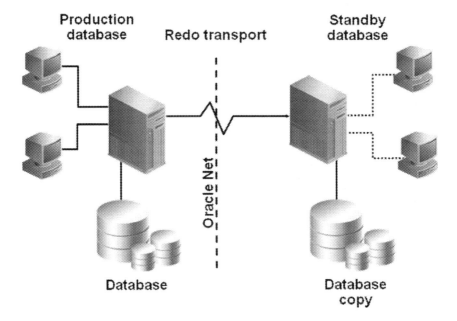

Production
database   Redo transport

Standby
database

Oracle Net

Database

Database
copy

V-2 TYPES OF STANDBY DATABASES

The standby databases are of two types:

- ➢ Physical standby database
- ➢ Logical standby database

➢ The physical standby database is identical (at the physical structure) to the primary base. The two databases have the same block size and the same name (db_name). The logs received are directly applied. It must be in MOUNT mode such that the application of logs is possible. It can be opened in read only mode, in which case the application of logs is interrupted.

In 11g versions, we have a special type of physical standby database called **snapshot standby database** which can be opened in READ/WRITE mode. In that kind of standby database, redo logs are received from the primary but are not applied. They will be applied when this snapshot standby database is converted back into a normal physical standby database. We also have in 11gR2, ACTIVE DATA GUARD which requires an additional license.

Oracle Active Data Guard enables read-only access to a physical standby database for queries, reporting, while continuously applying changes received from the production database.

➢ The logical standby database is different from the point of view of physical structure to the primary base. Thus, the log information received cannot be directly applied. They are first converted into SQL and then executed. This condition requires that the database be opened in read / write, reports and even DML and DDL instructions depending on the type of GUARD chosen are possible on this type of standby database, it has the disadvantage of not supporting all types of data.

Use a physical or logical standby database?

The answer depends on:

➤ The nature of your data
➤ The exploitation of the standby database.

Generally, a Data Guard configuration contains the two basic types of standby databases. Thus the logical standby is used for the production of reports, and the physical standby as it is identical to the primary base, for the rapid switchover or change in case of loss of the principal with minimal loss of data.

V-3 <u>DIFFERENT FIGURES OF TRANSFER</u>

PRIMARY DATABASE WITHOUT STANDBY DATABASE

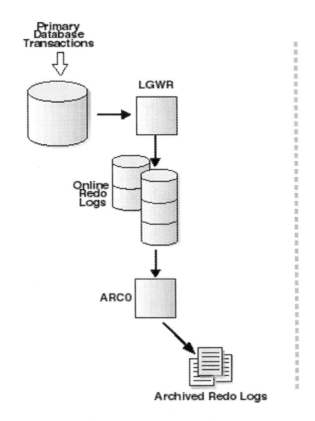

ASYNCHRONOUS TRANSMISSION

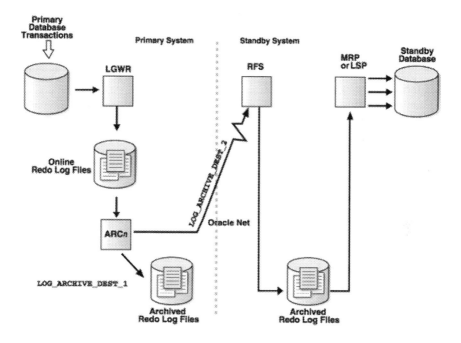

☞ After archiving on the primary site, data are applied in the standby database either by the process Managed Recovery Process (MRP) if physical base or by the Logical Standby process (LSP) if logical standby.

SYNCHRONOUS TRANSFER BY THE PROCESS LGWR TO REMOTE SITE

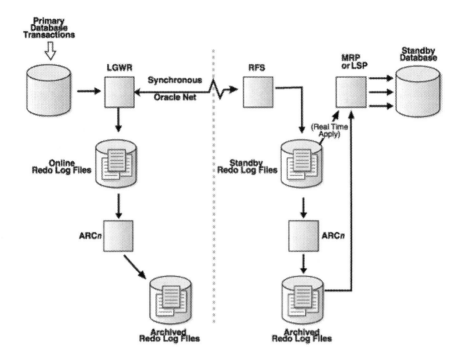

In this case, the LGWR process writes both redo log data locally on the main site and sends the data to the standby site that will be written by the process RFS (Remote File Server). The writing is first performed locally by default and is made synchronously. LGWR therefore expects that the writing be completed on the primary site before transferring the information to the standby site. This default behavior can be modified by selecting the asynchronous writing, in this case the remote network I/O are carried out without waiting for the end of writing by LGWR. The data sent by the latter is first routed through the LNSn process (LGWR Network Server) which then contacts the RFS process for remote write. If the standby redo logfiles exist on the standby site, redo log data are written in these files in lieu of being written directly to the archived logfiles.

The apply of data received in the standby database is always made (by MRP or LSP) after archiving at the main site, unless the real time

APPLY in has been enabled, in which case the application is made after validation on primary site as entries in the standby redo log. If the apply service is impossible (standby database in read only mode for example), the received data are automatically archived. The catch being done as soon as possible. The standby logfile and Real Time Apply will be detailed later in this book.

V-4 REQUIREMENTS FOR DATA GUARD: HARDWARE & OPERATING SYSTEM, RDBMS ORACLE

- The material can be different for the primary database and for standby database.
- The operating system must be the same on the primary database and standby database
- The versions of the OS may be different
- The same version of Oracle Database Enterprise must be installed for all databases
- The same types of files must be supported on both sites (if the primary site uses ASM or OMF files, the standby site should use this type also.)

V-5 DATA GUARD BROKER FEATURES

DATA GUARD BROKER is a distributed management structure that automates and centralizes the creation, updating and monitoring of Data Guard configurations. Through the broker, local management operations or remote ones can be done via friendly interfaces:

- Either online ordering DGMGRL
- Or via the Enterprise Manager Grid Control graphic

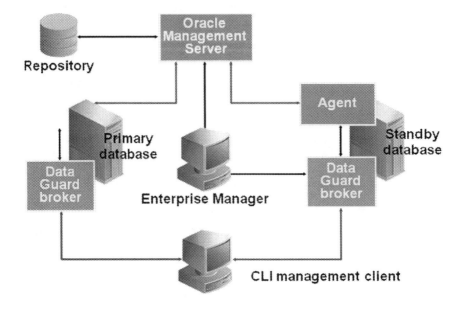

The components of Data Guard can be classified into two types:

Client-side components:

- Enterprise Manager Grid Control
- DGMGRL

The client can use Enterprise Manager from any computer with a browser and having access to Oracle Management Server; to use DGMGRL, Oracle client (minimum) must be installed.

Server-side components:

(That is to say, where is installed the database (primary or standby) as part of the Data Guard configuration).

- DMON process
- Configuration files

DMON (Data Guard Monitor) is a process running in the background on each site managed by the BROKER. The start of this process is done by assigning the value TRUE to initialization parameter DG_BROKER_START

DMON uses two configuration files defined by the initialization parameters DG_BROKER_CONFIG_FILE1 and DG_BROKER_CONFIG_FILE2 whose default values are $ORACLE_HOME/dbs/dr1 <SID>. dat and $ ORACLE_HOME/dbs/dr2 <SID>. dat.

Caution:

When creating the DATA GUARD BROKER by ENTERPRISE MANAGER, the value TRUE is automatically assigned to the parameter DG_BROKER_START on all instances of databases of the broker. On the otherhand, if you use the command line mode (DGMGRL), it must first be manually assigned to this parameter TRUE before ordering in the broker.

```
oracle@server1:~                                            _ □ ✕
File  Edit  View  Terminal  Tabs  Help
[oracle@server1 ~]$ dgmgrl
DGMGRL for Linux: Version 10.2.0.3.0 - Production

Copyright (c) 2000, 2005, Oracle. All rights reserved.

Welcome to DGMGRL, type "help" for information.
DGMGRL> help

The following commands are available:

add           Add a standby database to the broker configuration
connect       Connect to an Oracle instance
create        Create a broker configuration
disable       Disable a configuration, a database, or Fast-Start Failover
edit          Edit a configuration, database, or instance
enable        Enable a configuration, a database, or Fast-Start Failover
exit          Exit the program
failover      Change a standby database to be the primary database
help          Display description and syntax for a command
quit          Exit the program
reinstate     Change a disabled database into a viable standby database
rem           Comment to be ignored by DGMGRL
remove        Remove a configuration, database, or instance
show          Display information about a configuration, database, or instance
shutdown      Shutdown a currently running Oracle instance
start         Start Fast-Start Failover observer
startup       Start an Oracle database instance
stop          Stop Fast-Start Failover observer
switchover    Switch roles between the primary database and a standby database

Use "help <command>" to see syntax for individual commands

DGMGRL> connect sys/oracle@orcl
Connected.
Error:
ORA-16525: the Data Guard broker is not yet available
ORA-06512: at "SYS.DBMS_DRS", line 124
ORA-06512: at line 1

DGMGRL> ▮
```

Requirements for use of data guard broker

- The network file Oracle Net must be configured for instances of database in the configuration. This is done automatically if using Enterprise Manager, if not, this configuration must be done manually, and TCP/IP is required.

  Since version 8i Oracle database, registration of services at the listener is made dynamically to the listening port 1521, but in order to allow Data Guard broker to restart instances during the execution of Data Guard broker the operations, the registration of database services must be manual and the value assigned to the global name of the database during the registration must be equal to db_unique_name_DGMGRL.db_domain,

  db_unique_name: unique name of the database (by default equal to db _name)

  db _domaine: domain name of your network.

- The LOCAL_LISTENER parameter must be set in the Spfile when the primary database listener is using a non-standard port (not equal to 1521).

- The primary database must be in ARCHIVELOG mode

- In RAC mode, the settings dg _broker_config_filen must be redirected on the same files (shared) in all RAC instances and START_OPTIONS should be set to MOUNT in OCR repository (see RAC documentation for more details on SRVCTL command)

- The Use of the parameter file of type SPFILE is required to allow the broker to update the initialization parameter values in the database instance and the broker configuration file.

☞ To change initialization parameters when using the broker, it is recommended to use Enterprise Manager or the command line interface DGMGRL, to avoid receiving error messages about the status of Data Guard broker components.

CHAPTER 6

CREATING A PHYSICAL
STANDBY DATABASE

In this chapter, we will learn to create a physical standby database in 2 ways:

- By Enterprise Manager
- By RMAN and DGMGRL commands

VI-1 CREATION OF A PHYSICAL STANDBY DATABASE BY ENTERPRISE MANAGER

Enterprise Manager database control cannot manage Data Guard Broker. Using Enterprise Manager Grid Control is required.
The installation of Grid Control and the agents (OMS and OMA) is described in the Annex.

We will use Enterprise Manager to both create a DATA GUARD CONFIG BROKER and a standby database.

.

Before creating any type of standby database, it is recommended to activate the mode FORCE LOGGING on the primary database. In this mode, all changes to a database block are logged (except temporary tablespace blocks) even if NOLOGGING clause is used in some DDL or DML commands such as:

CREATE TABLE...   AS SELECT...   NOLOGGING
CREATE INDEX...   AS SELECT...   NOLOGGING
INSERT/ hint/...   AS SELECT...   NOLOGGING

Activation is made by the SQL command:

SQL>ALTER DATABASE FORCE LOGGING;

And verification of this mode is done by checking the column FORCE_
LOGGING of the view V$database

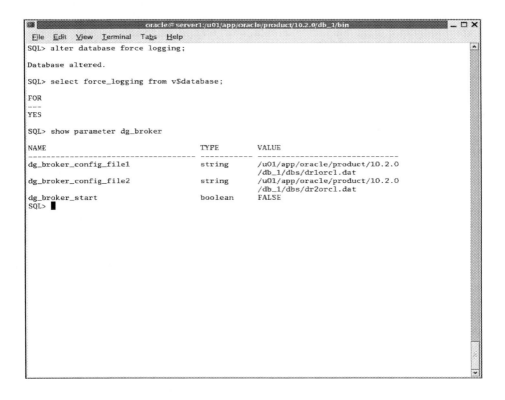

After placing the primary database in ARCHIVELOG mode, we start
the standby database wizard.

Images of creation of standby database by enterprise manager

Step 1) Activation of ARCHIVELOG MODE

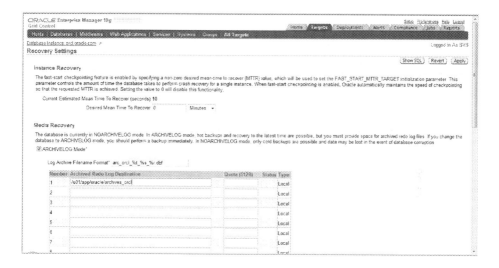

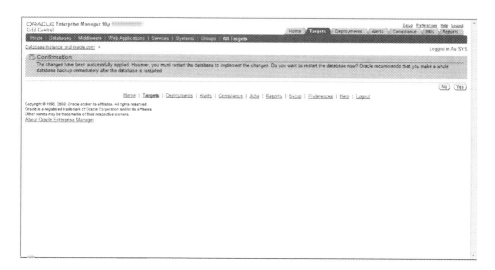

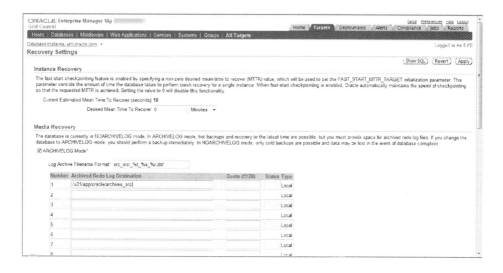

Step 2) Launching the standby wizard

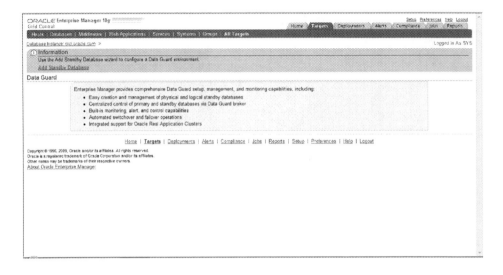

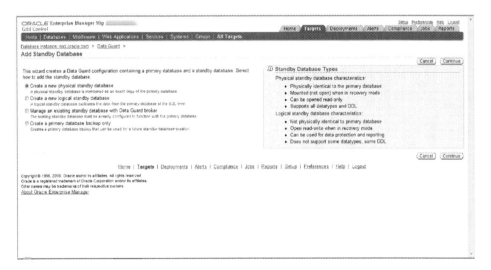

After clicking on CONTINUE on the page add standby database, wizard checks the following prerequisites:

- The primary database is started with the file SPFILE
- The database is in ARCHIVELOG mode
- The COMPATIBLE parameter is at least equal to 9.0.

It also verifies the FORCE LOGGING mode, but unlike the prerequisites above, does not generate an error if it is False, only a warning.

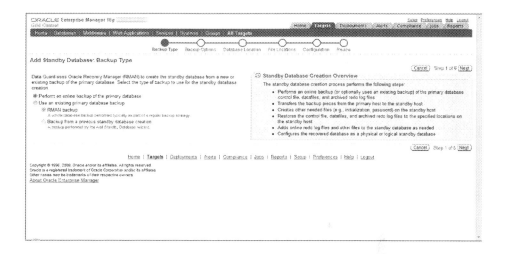

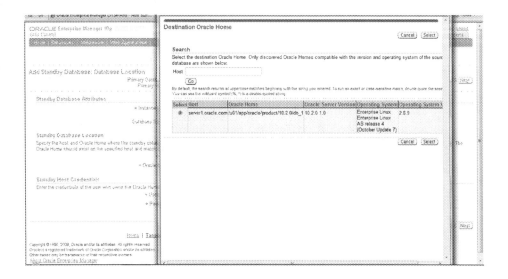

- The 10.2.0 version of Oracle software not being installed on the server2 where we want to create the standby database, the wizard cannot find it out.
- When we install version 10.2.0.1, modify the value of ORACLE HOME and bounce the listener, after stopping and restarting the agent on the server 2, the wizard discovers the host server 2.

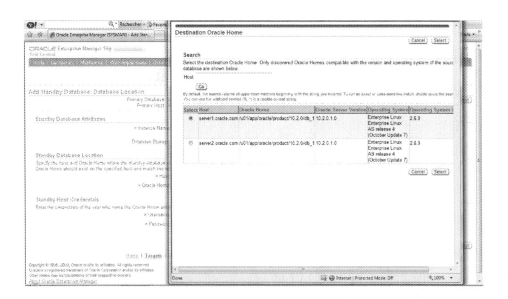

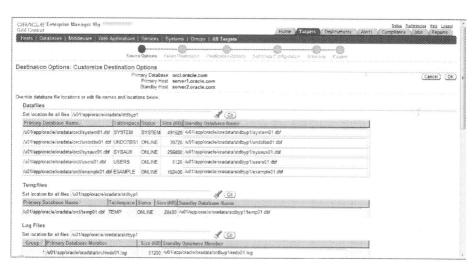

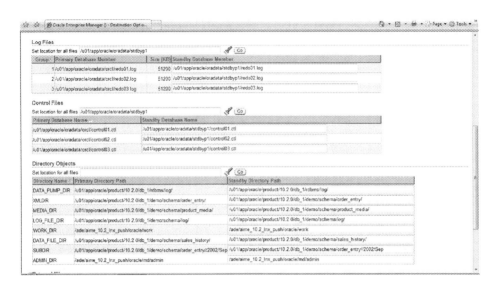

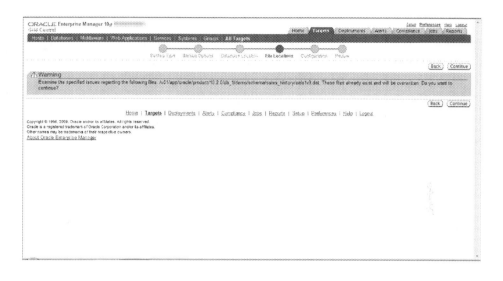

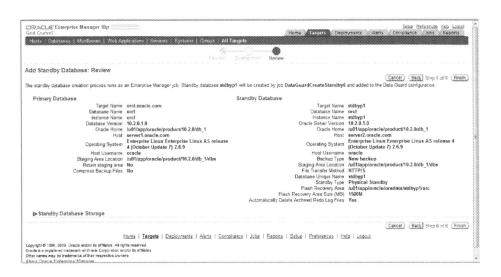

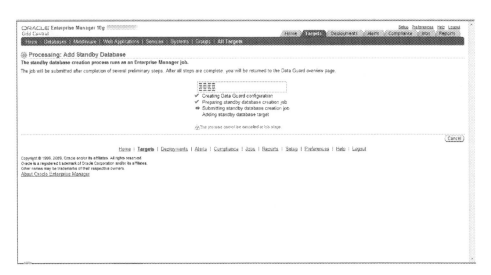

After creating the physical standby database, we check some initialization parameters and the static registration of the service with the listener.

```
# Listener47645.ora Network Configuration File: /
tmp/listener47645.ora
# Generated by Oracle configuration tools.
LISTENER_STDBYP1 =
   (DESCRIPTION =
      (ADDRESS = (PROTOCOL = TCP) (HOST = server2.
oracle.com) (PORT = 1522))
# Listener.ora Network Configuration File
# Created by Oracle Enterprise Manager Database Clone
tool

SID_LIST_LISTENER_STDBYP1 =
   (SID_LIST =
      (SID_DESC =
         (GLOBAL_DBNAME stdbyp1_DGMGRL.oracle.com =)
         (ORACLE_HOME=/u01/app/oracle/product/10.2.0/db_1)
         (SID_NAME = stdbyp1)
```

On the primary database, we make a switch of the logfile
```
SQL> ALTER SYSTEM SWITCH LOGFILE;
```

We see after a few moments in Enterprise Manager that the current log has been transmitted to the physical standby (sequence number 12)

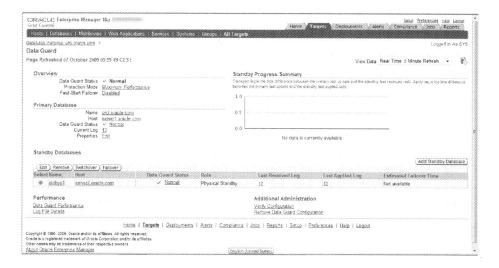

The configuration status of the broker can also be displayed with DGMGRL.

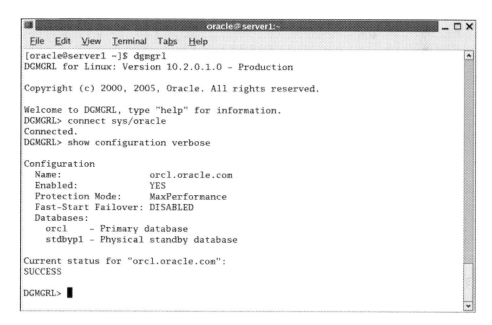

Verifying the Data Guard Configuration

In Enterprise Manager (and only with that Interface) we can verify the configuration of the Data Guard by just clicking on verify configuration in the section Additional Administration of Data Guard home page. The verification of the well health of the Data Guard broker is done by:

- Switching current log
- Updating Data Guard information
- Verifying protection mode
- Checking standby redo log files
- Checking Data Guard status
- Checking properties
- Verifying log switch

The results with details about the different steps are produced at the end of this verification

Sample of a verification

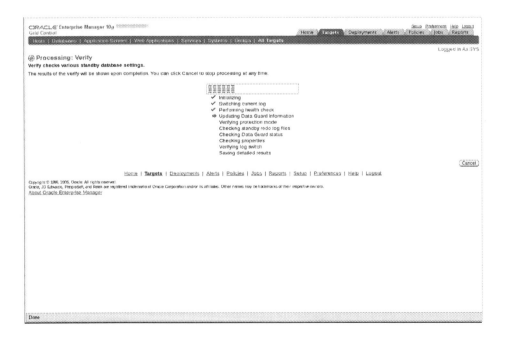

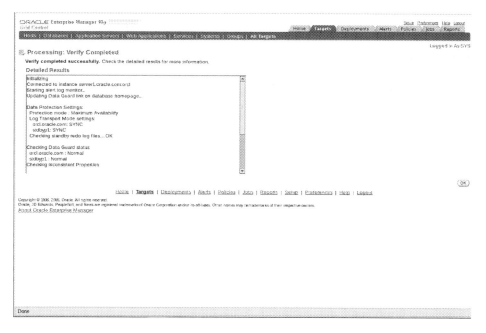

Resuming a standby database creation after a failure.

If a failure occurs during the creation of a standby database, before restarting a new creation, first clean up what have been already created by following:

-   Remove the configuration using DGMGRL
    DGMRGRL>Remove configuration;
-   Remove the entries of services in the listener using netmgr
-   Suppress the files created (data, redo, control, spfile . . .)
-   Remove the target standby database in Enterprise Manager
-   Remove the entry of the standby instance in /etc/oratab file (case of Linux system)
-   Kill the running Processes related to the standby instance (by $kill —9 PID)
    Where PID is the process ID.

VI-2 CREATION OF A PHYSICAL STANDBY DATABASE BY THE MANUAL PROCEDURE

The manual method is longer but offers better control over the configuration settings. The recommended approach is as follows:

1) Modification of the initialization parameter file of the primary site and creation of a initialization parameters file for the standby instance

2) Backup of data files from the primary database (do not save redo logfiles)

3) Creation of a control file for standby database

4) Copy of files saved in steps 2 and 3 plus the Initialization parameter file created in step 1 to the system hosting the standby database

5) Creation of a service (if using Windows Operating System) on the standby site

6) Creation of a password file on the standby site

7) Configuration of Oracle Net files (listener, tnsnames)

8) Creation of the standby database through RMAN DUPLICATE command

9) Start the LOG APPLY on the physical standby database

1) Initialization parameters file

orcl.__db_cache_size = 364904448

orcl.__java_pool_size = 4194304

orcl.__large_pool_size = 4194304

orcl.__shared_pool_size = 159383552

orcl.__streams_pool_size = 0

*.Archive_lag_target = 0

*.Audit_file_dest = '/ u01/app/oracle/admin/orcl/adump'

*. Background_dump_dest = '/ u01/app/oracle/admin/orcl/bdump'

*. Compatible = '10.2.0.1.0'

*. Control_files = '/ u01/app/oracle/oradata/orcl/control01.ctl', '/ u01/app/oracle/oradata/orcl/control02.ctl', '/u01/app/oracle/oradata/ orcl / control03.ctl'

*. Core_dump_dest = '/ u01/app/oracle/admin/orcl/cdump'

*.DB_BLOCK_SIZE = 8192

*. Db_domain = 'oracle.com'

*.Db_file_multiblock_read_count = 16

*. Db_name = 'orcl'

*. Db_recovery_file_dest = '/ u01/app/oracle/flash_recovery_area'

*. Db_recovery_file_dest_size = 2147483648

*.Dg_broker_start = TRUE

*. Dispatchers = '(PROTOCOL = TCP) (SERVICE = orclXDB)'

*.Job_queue_processes = 10

*. Log_archive_config = 'dg_config = (stdbyp1)'

*. Log_archive_dest_1 = 'LOCATION = / u01/app/oracle/archives_ orcl OPTIONAL reopen = 300'

*. Log_archive_dest_10 = 'LOCATION = USE_DB_RECOVERY_ FILE_DEST OPTIONAL reopen = 300'

orcl.log_archive_dest_1 ='location ="/ u01/app/oracle/archives_orcl"', 'valid_for = (ONLINE_LOGFILE, ALL_ROLES)'

*. Log_archive_dest_2 = 'service = "(DESCRIPTION = (ADDRESS_ LIST = (ADDRESS = (PROTOCOL =TCP) (HOST = server2.oracle. com) (PORT = 1522))) (CONNECT_DATA = (SERVICE_NAME = stdbyp1_XPT.oracle.com) (instance_name = stdbyp1) (SERVER = Dedicated)))"',' ARCH SYNC Noaffirmation delay = 0 OPTIONAL max_failure = 0 max_connections = 1 reopen = 300 db_unique_name = "stdbyp1" register net_timeout valid_for = 180 = (online_logfile, primary_role)'

orcl.log_archive_dest_state_1 = 'ENABLE'

*. Log_archive_dest_state_2 = 'ENABLE'

*. Log_archive_format = '% t_% s_ arc_orcl_ r.dbf%'

orcl.log_archive_format = '% t_% s_ arc_orcl_ r.dbf%'

*.Log_archive_max_processes = 2

*.Log_archive_min_succeed_dest = 1

orcl.log_archive_trace = 0

*.Open_cursors = 300

*.Pga_aggregate_target = 201326592

*. Processes = 150

*. Remote_login_passwordfile = 'EXCLUSIVE'

*.Sga_target = 536870912

orcl.standby_archive_dest ="

*. Standby_file_management = 'AUTO'

*. Undo_management = 'AUTO'

*. Undo_tablespace = 'UNDOTBS1'

*. User_dump_dest = '/ u01/app/oracle/admin/orcl/udump'

1) **Modification of the initialization parameter file of the primary database**

We create a file pfile from the SPFile to modify it and use it for the standby site.

```
SQL> CREATE PFILE = '/home/oracle/pfileorcl.ora'
from SPFile;
```

- DB_UNIQUE_NAME: Unique global name for the database is by default equal to db_name, replaces the old setting lock_name_space which has become obsolete.

  In a Data Guard environment with a physical standby database (the primary database and the standby have the same db _name), in this case each instance must have a distinct separate value db_unique_name

- LOG_ARCHIVE_DEST_n $n \in [1,10] \rightarrow$ in V10g

  $n \in [1.31] \rightarrow$ in V11g

In addition to local destination (s), specify at least one remote destination for archiving through standby database by specifying the SERVICE and DB_UNIQUE_NAME terms in the parameter LOG _ARCHIVE_DEST_n

Simplified Format

LOG_ARCHIVE_DEST_n ='Service = service _name VALID_FOR = (log_type, role_type) DB_unique_name =unique_name of_standby'

Service_name : Configured service network via Oracle Net, must match with the instance of the Standby Database.

VALID_FOR: Specifies when RFS can transmit redo data depending on the type of redo log and the database role.

Possible combinations

COMBINATION	PRIMARY BASE	PHYSICAL BASE	LOGICAL BASE
Online_logfile, Primary_ role	Valid	ignored*	ignored
Online_logfile, Standby _role	ignored	ignored	Valid
Online_logfile, All_roles	Valid	ignored	Valid
Standby_ logfile-Standby_role	ignored	Valid	Valid
Standby_logfile-All_ roles	Ignored	Valid	Valid
All_logfiles, Primary_role	Valid	ignored	ignored
All_logfiles, Standby_role	ignored	Valid	Valid
All_logfiles, All_roles**	Valid	Valid	Valid

Comments:

*A physical standby database does not use online Redo logfiles because it cannot be opened in READ-WRITE, unless it is converted into a snapshot standby database in 11g version only.

**Default value, but not recommended may lead to a wrong archiving when changing the database role.

***The order of the combination does not matter

Some attributes of the parameter LOG_ARCHIVE_DEST_n

MANDATORY Archiving must be successful in this location before the redo log online can be reused

MAX FAILURE: number of times an attempt is made on a location in failure. Beyond this number, the location is considered failure, and the location specified by ALTERNATE is USED.

REOPEN (default 300s): minimum time before retry

NET TIMEOUT: number of seconds the LGWR waits for the status of LNS before terminating a connection (default 180)

ALTERNATE: backup location in case of failure of the primary location, if specified, reopen must be set to 0 or a value must be assigned to MAX_FAILURE

If REOPEN=0 then
Failed destinations remain disabled until manual reactivation by :
(SQL>alter SYSTEM set LOG_ARCHIVE_DEST_STATE_n = ENABLE)
or are automatically reactivated when you restart the instance.

MAX CONNECTIONS: defines the number of connections used to transmit redo logfiles archives to a remote destination (default 1). To do this,

LOG_ARCHIVE_MAX_PROCESSES must be greater or equal to MAX_CONNECTIONS and LOG_ARCHIVE_ LOCAL_FIRST must be True, which is its default value.

DELAY specifies in minutes the time between archiving logs on physical standby database and the application of this archive, it is ignored if mode is Real Time Apply, default 30 minutes.

Other attributes of parameter LOG_ARCHIVE_DEST_n such as SYNC / ASYNC, ARCH / LGWR will be seen in the chapter "Protection Mode"

DB_FILE_NAME_CONVERT,   LOG_FILE_NAME_CONVERT
Specify these parameters on the standby database when the location of data files or redo logfiles in the primary database differ from those of the Standby Database. Must contain an even number of values.

- STANDBY_FILE_MANAGEMENT (AUTO | MANUAL) to be defined both in the primary database and standby database. When it is AUTO, the operations of the replacement of the file name, adding, deleting a log file or file creation are prohibited on the standby database.
  If MANUAL (default value), files created on the primary database are not added automatically to the standby database, copy them manually.
- FAL_SERVER, FAL_CLIENT: to be defined only in case of physical standby database on both the primary and the standby database.
    On the primary database

    FAL_SERVER = Oracle Net entry of standby database.
    FAL_CLIENT = Oracle Net entry of primary database
    On the standby database, the two values are swapped

- STANDBY_ARCHIVE_DEST: to be defined solely on the Standby Database. Specifies the directory where the archive logs are created. Overrides the location specified in the parameter LOG_ARCHIVE_DEST_n

2) Backup of files on the primary database

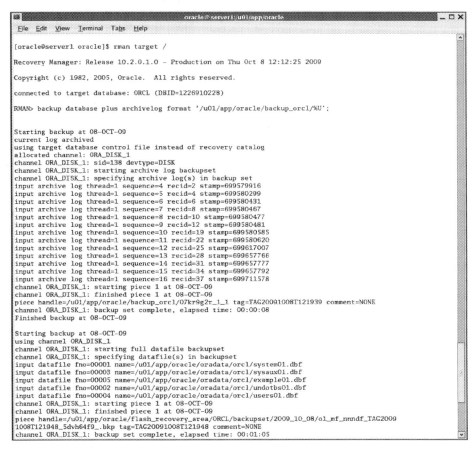

We perform the RMAN backup.

3) Creation of the control file for the standby database

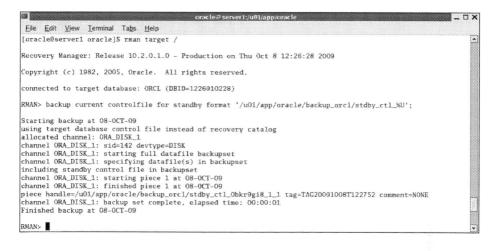

4) Copy the files created in steps 1 to 3 on the standby system

☞ **NB** The data files and control files created by RMAN must be copied on the backup system in the backup location of the source system.

☞ If in Version 11, this copy is no longer necessary. In our case in these files must be placed in /u01/ app/oracle/backup_orcl

```
oracle@server2:/u01/app/oracle/backup_orcl                          _ □ ×
File  Edit  View  Terminal  Tabs  Help
[oracle@server1 oracle]$ ssh server2
The authenticity of host 'server2 (192.168.0.2)' can't be established.
RSA key fingerprint is 5a:d7:e9:e6:2a:51:0a:a5:55:c3:7b:5c:70:58:4e:c9.
Are you sure you want to continue connecting (yes/no)? yes
Warning: Permanently added 'server2,192.168.0.2' (RSA) to the list of known hosts.
oracle@server2's password:
Last login: Tue Oct  6 22:36:00 2009
-bash: /u01/app/oracle/product/10.2.0/db_1/jdk/jre/lib/i386/server:: Aucun fichier ou répertoire de ce type
-bash: /u01/app/oracle/product/10.2.0/db_1/rdbms/lib:/u01/app/oracle/product/10.2.0/db_1/lib:/u01/app/oracle/
product/10.2.0/db_1/jdk/jre/lib/i386:: Aucun fichier ou répertoire de ce type
[oracle@server2 ~]$ cd /u01/app/oracle/
[oracle@server2 oracle]$ mkdir backup_orcl
[oracle@server2 oracle]$ cd backup_orcl/
[oracle@server2 backup_orcl]$ scp server1:/u01/app/oracle/backup_orcl/* .
07kr9g2r_1_1                                    100%   79MB   8.8MB/s   00:09
0akr9g58_1_1                                    100%  110KB 110.0KB/s   00:00
stdby_ctl_0bkr9gi8_1_1                          100% 7168KB   7.0MB/s   00:00
[oracle@server2 backup_orcl]$ ▮
```

The initialization parameter file for the physical standby database created at in step 1 is then copied to the backup system.

5) If in a Windows system only, create the service using the command ORADIM

```
C:> ORADIM — new—SID sid —SRVC srvc —STARTMODE
auto|manual — SPFILE . . .
```

6) Creation of the password file in the standby system

☞ Note: This file must contain the same password as that of the primary instance.

```
orapwd file=$ORACLE_HOME/dbs/orapwstdby11
password=oracle
```

7) Configuration of Oracle Net files on the primary and standby systems

7-1 Register statically the services in the listener and create an entry for the primary instance in tnsnames.ora of the host server2

$ netmgr

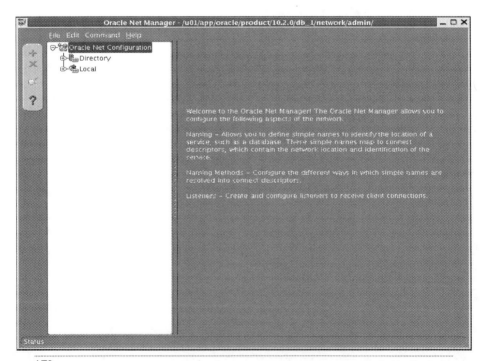

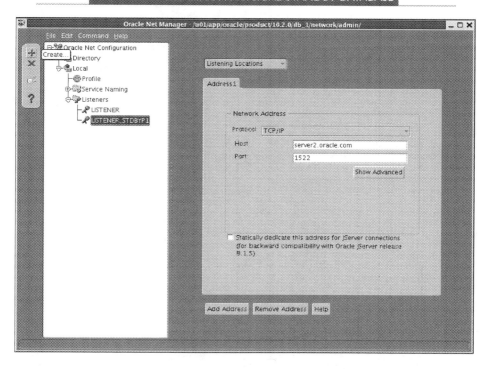

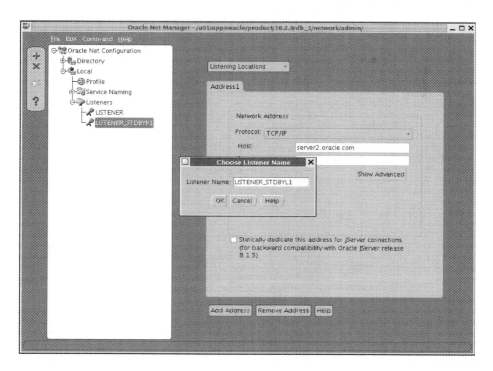

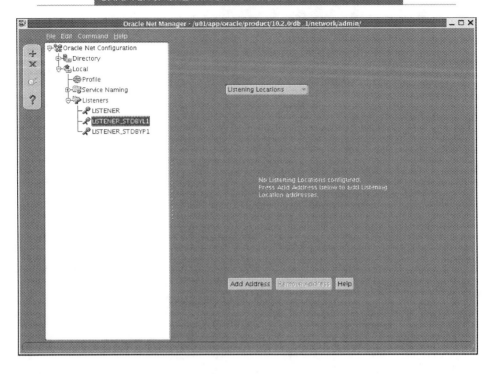

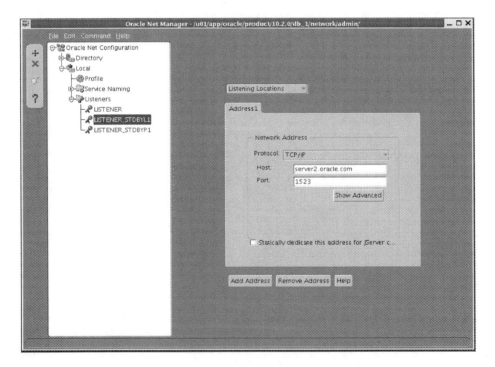

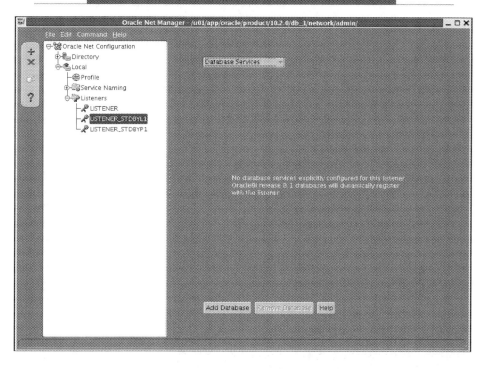

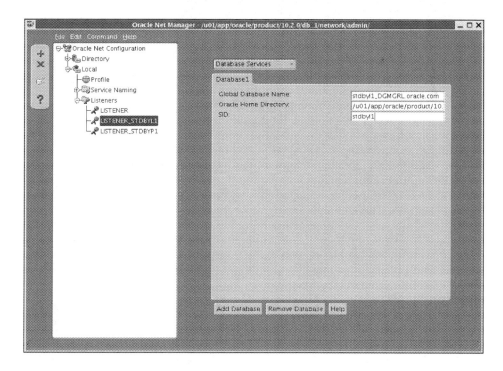

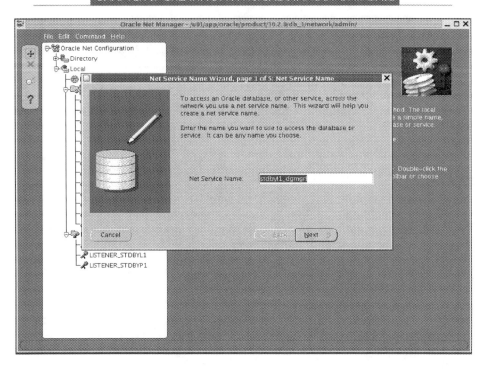

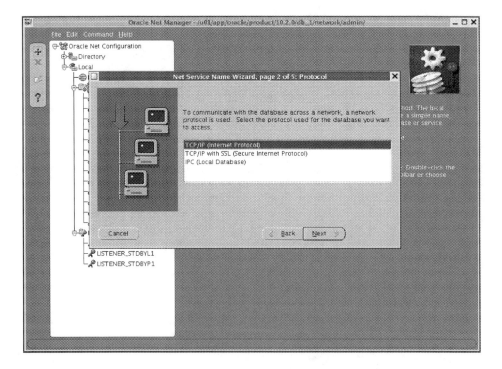

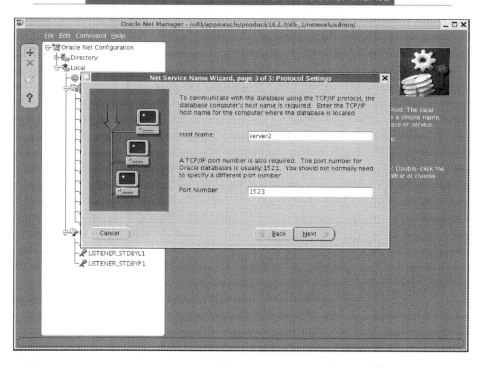

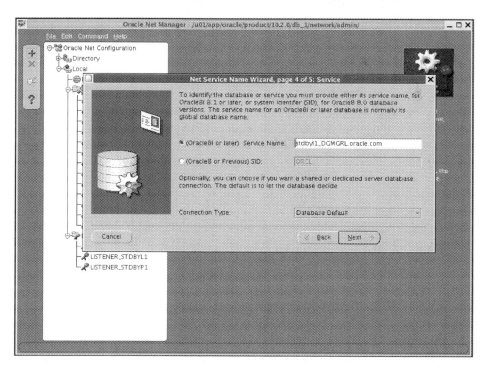

Note: Netmgr version 10.2.0.1 does not support the service names of more than 8 characters without counting domain name (a patch is required for that), if you have that release, manually edit the file tnsnames. ora, to add the network service stdbyl1_DGMGRL
tnsnames65173.ora Network Configuration File: /tmp/tnsnames65173.ora
Generated by Oracle configuration tools.

```
LISTENER_STDBYP1 =
  (ADDRESS = (PROTOCOL = TCP)(HOST = server2.oracle.
  com)(PORT = 1522))
LISTENER_STDBYL1 =
  (ADDRESS = (PROTOCOL = TCP)(HOST = server2.oracle.
  com)(PORT = 1523))
#TNSNAMES.ORA Network Configuration File
#Created by Oracle Enterprise Manager Clone Database
tool
STDBYP1_DGMGRL =
  (DESCRIPTION =
    (ADDRESS_LIST =
      (ADDRESS = (PROTOCOL = TCP)(HOST = server2.
      oracle.com)(PORT = 1522))
)
    (CONNECT_DATA =
      (SERVICE_NAME = stdbyp1_DGMGRL.oracle.com)
STDBYL1_DGMGRL =
  (DESCRIPTION =
    (ADDRESS_LIST =
      (ADDRESS = (PROTOCOL = TCP)(HOST= server2.
      oracle.com)(PORT = 1523))
    (CONNECT_DATA =
      (SERVICE_NAME = stdbyl1_DGMGRL.oracle.com)
    ) )
```

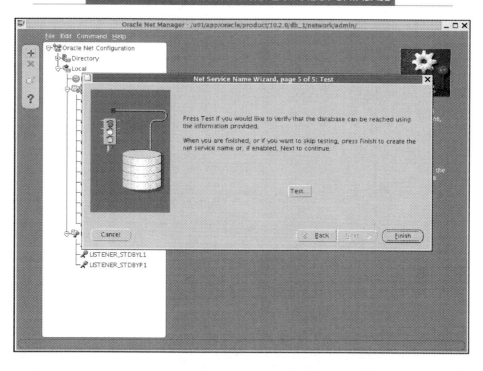

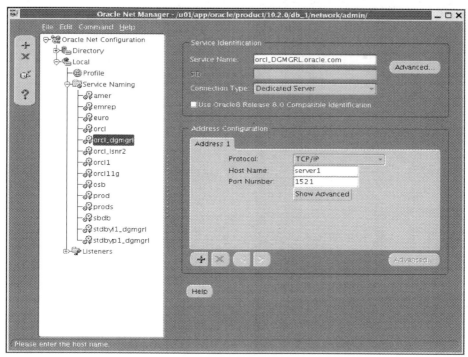

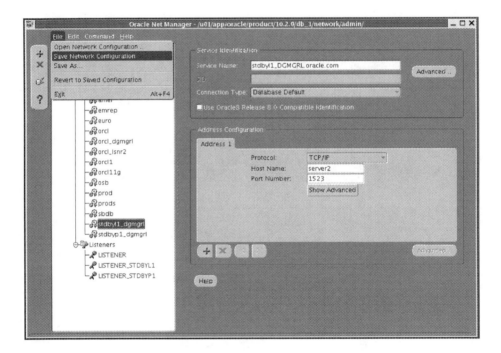

Stop and restart the listener on standby site

```
                              oracle@server2:~                        _ □ ×
Fichier   Édition   Affichage   Terminal   Onglets   Aide
LSNRCTL> status listener_stdbyp1
Connecting to (DESCRIPTION=(ADDRESS=(PROTOCOL=TCP)(HOST=server2.oracle.com)(PORT
=1522)))
STATUS of the LISTENER
------------------------
Alias                     listener_stdbyp1
Version                   TNSLSNR for Linux: Version 10.2.0.1.0 - Production
Start Date                08-OCT-2009 13:15:02
Uptime                    0 days 1 hr. 46 min. 19 sec
Trace Level               off
Security                  ON: Local OS Authentication
SNMP                      OFF
Listener Parameter File   /u01/app/oracle/product/10.2.0/db_1/network/admin/list
ener.ora
Listener Log File         /u01/app/oracle/product/10.2.0/db_1/network/log/listen
er_stdbyp1.log
Listening Endpoints Summary...
  (DESCRIPTION=(ADDRESS=(PROTOCOL=tcp)(HOST=server2.oracle.com)(PORT=1522)))
Services Summary...
Service "stdbyp1.oracle.com" has 1 instance(s).
  Instance "stdbyp1", status READY, has 1 handler(s) for this service...
Service "stdbyp1_DGB.oracle.com" has 1 instance(s).
  Instance "stdbyp1", status READY, has 1 handler(s) for this service...
Service "stdbyp1_DGMGRL.oracle.com" has 1 instance(s).
  Instance "stdbyp1", status UNKNOWN, has 1 handler(s) for this service...
Service "stdbyp1_XPT.oracle.com" has 1 instance(s).
  Instance "stdbyp1", status READY, has 1 handler(s) for this service...
The command completed successfully
LSNRCTL> status listener_stdby11
Connecting to (DESCRIPTION=(ADDRESS=(PROTOCOL=TCP)(HOST=server2.oracle.com)(PORT
=1523)))
TNS-12541: TNS:no listener
 TNS-12560: TNS:protocol adapter error
  TNS-00511: No listener
   Linux Error: 111: Connection refused
LSNRCTL> start listener_stdby11
Starting /u01/app/oracle/product/10.2.0/db_1/bin/tnslsnr: please wait...

TNSLSNR for Linux: Version 10.2.0.1.0 - Production
System parameter file is /u01/app/oracle/product/10.2.0/db_1/network/admin/liste
ner.ora
Log messages written to /u01/app/oracle/product/10.2.0/db_1/network/log/listener
_stdby11.log
Listening on: (DESCRIPTION=(ADDRESS=(PROTOCOL=tcp)(HOST=server2.oracle.com)(PORT
=1523)))

Connecting to (DESCRIPTION=(ADDRESS=(PROTOCOL=TCP)(HOST=server2.oracle.com)(PORT
=1523)))
STATUS of the LISTENER
Alias                     listener_stdby11
Version                   TNSLSNR for Linux: Version 10.2.0.1.0 - Production
Start Date                08-OCT-2009 15:02:14
Uptime                    0 days 0 hr. 0 min. 0 sec
```

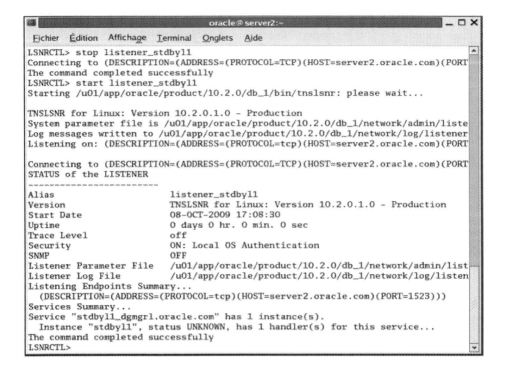

7-2) Repeat the same steps for static registration of the services in the listener and entry creation in tnsnames.ora for standby instance on host server1

8) Creation of the physical standby database

Some initialization parameters (as db_unique_name) added as static, we must restart the primary instance from pfile.

```
SQL>shutdown immediate;
SQL> create spfile from pfile='/home/oracle/initorcl.
ora'; THEN
SQL> STARTUP
```

8-a) creation of an auxiliary instance on the standby system.

```
oracle@server2:/u01/app/oracle/product/10.2.0/db_1/network/admin          _ □ X

Fichier  Édition  Affichage  Terminal  Onglets  Aide
[oracle@server2 admin]$ export ORACLE_SID=stdby11
[oracle@server2 admin]$ sqlplus sys/oracle as sysdba

SQL*Plus: Release 10.2.0.1.0 - Production on Thu Oct 8 17:45:07 2009

Copyright (c) 1982, 2005, Oracle.  All rights reserved.

Connected to an idle instance.

SQL> create spfile from pfile='/home/oracle/pfilestdby11.ora';

File created.

SQL> startup nomount
ORACLE instance started.

Total System Global Area  536870912 bytes
Fixed Size                  1220432 bytes
Variable Size             150995120 bytes
Database Buffers          381681664 bytes
Redo Buffers                2973696 bytes
SQL>
```

8-b) creation of the standby database

```
oracle@server1:~                                                          _ □ X

File  Edit  View  Terminal  Tabs  Help
With the Partitioning, OLAP and Data Mining options
[oracle@server1 ~]$ clear screen

[oracle@server1 ~]$ rman target /

Recovery Manager: Release 10.2.0.1.0 - Production on Thu Oct 8 17:48:56 2009

Copyright (c) 1982, 2005, Oracle.  All rights reserved.

connected to target database: ORCL (DBID=1226910228)

RMAN> connect auxiliary sys/oracle@stdby11

connected to auxiliary database: ORCL (not mounted)

RMAN> duplicate target database for standby
2> ;

Starting Duplicate Db at 08-OCT-09
using target database control file instead of recovery catalog
allocated channel: ORA_AUX_DISK_1
channel ORA_AUX_DISK_1: sid=154 devtype=DISK

contents of Memory Script:
{
   restore clone standby controlfile;
   sql clone 'alter database mount standby database';
}
executing Memory Script

Starting restore at 08-OCT-09
using channel ORA_AUX_DISK_1

channel ORA_AUX_DISK_1: starting datafile backupset restore
channel ORA_AUX_DISK_1: restoring control file
channel ORA_AUX_DISK_1: reading from backup piece /u01/app/oracle/backup_orcl/st
dby_ctl_0bkr9gi8_1_1
channel ORA_AUX_DISK_1: restored backup piece 1
piece handle=/u01/app/oracle/backup_orcl/stdby_ctl_0bkr9gi8_1_1 tag=TAG2009100BT
122752
channel ORA_AUX_DISK_1: restore complete, elapsed time: 00:00:04
output filename=/u01/app/oracle/oradata/stdby11/control01.ctl
output filename=/u01/app/oracle/oradata/stdby11/control02.ctl
output filename=/u01/app/oracle/oradata/stdby11/control03.ctl
Finished restore at 08-OCT-09

sql statement: alter database mount standby database
released channel: ORA_AUX_DISK_1

contents of Memory Script:
{
   set newname for tempfile  1 to
 "/u01/app/oracle/oradata/stdby11/temp01.dbf";
   switch clone tempfile all;
```

At the end of the duplicate command, the physical standby database is in mode MOUNT, but the LOG Apply is not started. You can check that by querying the V$managed_standby view on the standby database (The column PROCESS does not contain any MRP) or in UNIX/LINUX systems by checking if there is any mrp process related to the standby instance running by issuing ($ ps — ef | grep mrp).

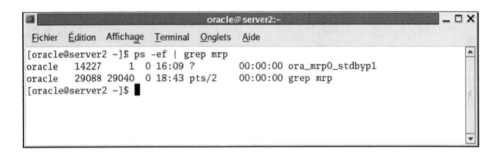

To check by SQL the status of the database and if a MRP process is running:

SQL> select open_mode from v$database;

OPEN_MODE

MOUNTED

SQL> select process,status,client_process from v$managed_standby;

PROCESS   STATUS   CLIENT_P
-------   ---------   --------
ARCH   CONNECTED   ARCH
ARCH   CONNECTED   ARCH

Start the apply of logs by

SQL> ALTER DATABASE RECOVER MANAGED STANDBY DATABASE [USING CURRENT LOGFILE] [NOPARALLEL] [DISCONNECT]

Remarks:

- Clause NOPARALLEL is obsolete in version 11g; the recovery will always be done in parallel.
- The clause USING CURRENT LOG FILE is specified if you want the application of logs to be done in real time. In this case it is necessary for the database to have standby redo logfiles.
- The clause DISCONNECT allows the process to be executed in the background, if not mentioned, the SQL session will not return the hand.

Addition of the standby database in the broker

The standby database being created, we now add it in the broker. Here we choose the method by command line.

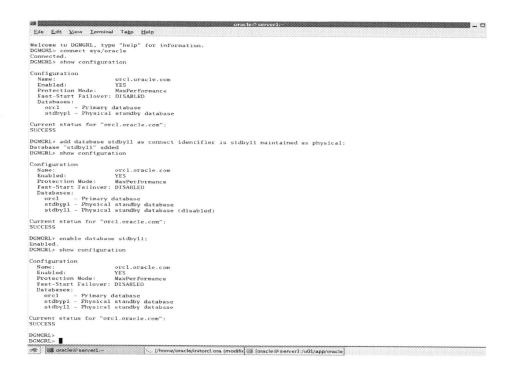

Caution: After adding a database in the broker, its status is disabled. Do not forget to activate it before use.

In the Data Guard broker, we see the primary database and the two standby databases while in the databases tab of Enterprise Manager, we do not see the newly created standby L1. This is normal, because the agent does not automatically discover the new targets added outside of Enterprise Manager.

For the display we can proceed in 2 ways either by:

1—Rediscovery of targets on the server2 by $AGENT_HOME / bin/ agentca—d

or

2—Adding database in the database page by clicking on add

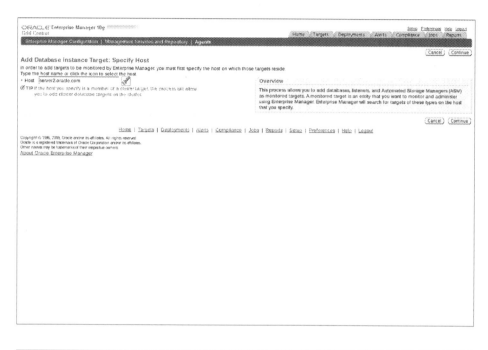

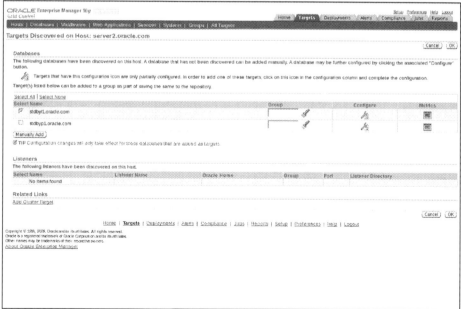

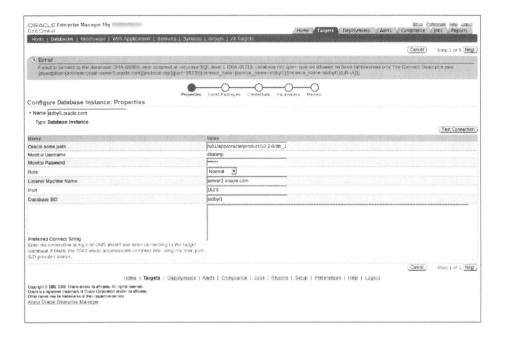

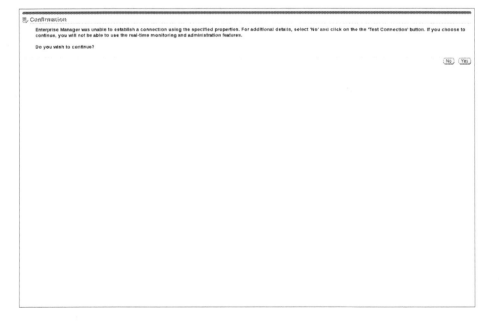

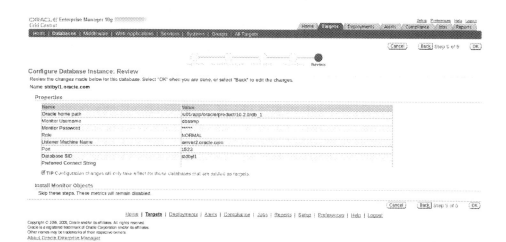

Configure Database Instance. Review

Review the changes made below for this database. Select "OK" when you are done, or select "Back" to edit the changes.

Name stdby1.oracle.com

Properties

Name	Value
Oracle home path	/u01/app/oracle/product/10.2.0/db_1
Monitor Username	dbsnmp
Monitor Password	*******
Role	NORMAL
Listener Machine Name	server2.oracle.com
Port	1523
Database SID	stdby1
Preferred Connect String	

☞ TIP Configuration changes will only have effect for those databases that are added as targets.

Install Monitor Objects

Skip these steps. These metrics will remain disabled.

Cancel   Back Step 5 of 5   OK

⊕ Database Instance Configuration Result

Target saving is in progress.

This operation may take several minutes. This page will automatically forward to the next page when done.

Target saving is in progress. This may take several minutes.

☞ TIP This operation cannot be cancelled. It will continue even if the browser window is closed.

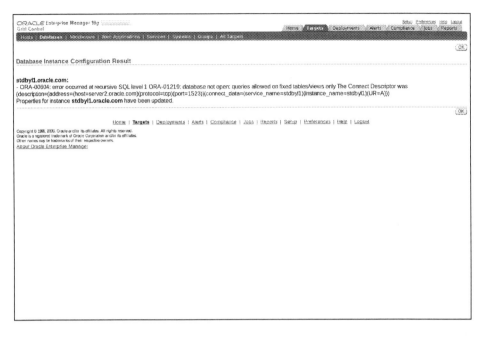

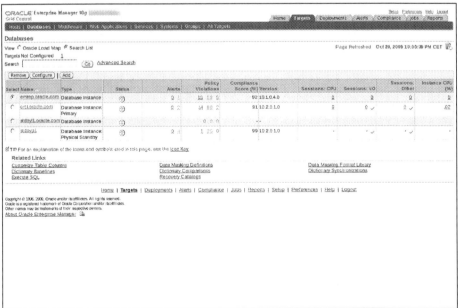

## CHAPTER 7

CREATION OF A LOGICAL STANDBY DATABASE

As we have seen in the introduction, a logical standby database must be opened in read / write for the SQL apply to be done. It thus offers advantages over the physical standby database (standard type) that must be in MOUNT mode to for apply of redo logfiles:

- Requests can be made on the logicial standby database thus relieving the primary database.
- The physical block corruptions on the primary database are not propagated to the logical standby database.

The logical standby database being opened in READ / WRITE, the changes can be made, making it not synchronized with the primary database. To avoid this, the DBA provides the command

```
SQL> ALTER DATABASE GUARD {ALL|STANDBY|NONE}
```

To monitor changes on the logical standby database.
ALL: Only the SYS user can modify data.
Mode enabled by default while creating a logical standby database from Data Guard BROKER.
STANDBY: Data updating by the service SQL Apply cannot be changed
NONE: Any user with privileges on the data can change them.

OBJECTS NOT SUPPORTED BY A LOGICAL STANDBY DATABASE

- Tables and sequences belonging to SYS schema
- Tables using table compression
- Materialized views
- Global temporary tables
- Tables containing data types not supported below:
  - BFILE
  - VARRAY, Nested Tables
  - ROWID, UROWID
  - User Defined Types
  - Types objet Ref (in 10g)
  - XML Standard
  - Spatial data

The tables containing these datatypes can be got by querying DBA_ LOGSTDBY_UNSUPPORTED View on the Primary database.

DDL STATEMENTS NOT TAKEN IN CHARGE

The following commands, executed on the primary database are not propagated to the logical standby database:

ALTER{DATABASE | SESSION | SYSTEM | MATERIALIZED VIEW| MATERIALIZED VIEW LOG}
CREATE {ControlFile | Database | Database LINK| Pfile FROM SPILE | SPFILE FROM PFILE | MATERIALIZED VIEW | MATERIALIZED VIEW LOG|SCHEMA AUTHORIZATION}
DROP {DATABASE LINK | MATERIALIZED VIEW |MATERIALIZED VIEW LOG} LOCK TABLE
EXPLAIN
SET CONTRAINTS
SET ROLE
SET Transactions

Caution

The execution of these commands on the primary database may stop the of SQL APPLY on the standby database. The DBA must in this case identify the instruction, re-run it on the logical standby database and restart the service APPLY.

CAN THE TABLES LINES OF THE PRIMARY DATABASE BE IDENTIFIED ON UNIQUE WAY?

Unlike the physical standby database, the logical standby database is not identical (in the physical point of view) to the primary database. Thus, the ROWID contained in the redo generated on the primary database can't be used to identify the corresponding row on the logical standby database. Another mechanism of mapping must be found. For this, we can use a primary key or unique index when possible.

We check the view DBA_LOGSTDBY_NOT_UNIQUE to obtain the tables without primary key or unique index for NOT NULL columns.

```
SQL> desc DBA_LOGSTDBY_NOT_UNIQUE
NAME            NULL          TYPE
-----------------------------------
OWNER
TABLE_NAME
BAD_COLUMN
```

Bad_Column can take two values: Y | N
Y: the type of data is unlimited (e.g. CLOB)
N: data type has limits
When BAD_COLUMN is N, we can add a primary key constraint on the table. It is advisable to use the RELY DISABLE clause resulting in less overhead in the system, because the validations are not made at any change on the table.

☞ These three limitations make that the logical standby database cannot always be changed with the primary database without losing data.

STEPS FOR CREATING A LOGICAL STANBY DATABASE

As for the physical standby database, there are two methods of creating the logical standby database:

- By Enterprise Manager
- By RMAN and DGMGRL / SQL commands

We describe below the steps to create by SQL / DGMGRL; the Enterprise Manager method is similar to the physical standby database.

PRIOR TASKS

1. On the primary database, identify data types not supported

```
oracle@server1:~                                                    _ □ ✕
File  Edit  View  Terminal  Tabs  Help
SQL> set lines 200
SQL> select owner,table_name,column_name,data_type from dba_logstdby_unsupported order by 1;

OWNER            TABLE_NAME            COLUMN_NAME                DATA_TYPE
---------------  --------------------  -------------------------  ----------------------
OE               CUSTOMERS             CUST_ADDRESS               CUST_ADDRESS_TYP
OE               CATEGORIES_TAB        PARENT_CATEGORY_ID         NUMBER
OE               CUSTOMERS             CUST_GEO_LOCATION          SDO_GEOMETRY
OE               WAREHOUSES            WAREHOUSE_SPEC             XMLTYPE
OE               WAREHOUSES            WH_GEO_LOCATION            SDO_GEOMETRY
OE               CUSTOMERS             PHONE_NUMBERS              PHONE_LIST_TYP
OE               CATEGORIES_TAB        CATEGORY_ID                NUMBER
OE               CATEGORIES_TAB        CATEGORY_DESCRIPTION       VARCHAR2
OE               CATEGORIES_TAB        CATEGORY_NAME              VARCHAR2
PM               ONLINE_MEDIA          PRODUCT_THUMBNAIL          ORDIMAGE
PM               ONLINE_MEDIA          PRODUCT_VIDEO              ORDVIDEO

OWNER            TABLE_NAME            COLUMN_NAME                DATA_TYPE
---------------  --------------------  -------------------------  ----------------------
PM               PRINT_MEDIA           AD_TEXTDOCS_NTAB           TEXTDOC_TAB
PM               PRINT_MEDIA           AD_GRAPHIC                 BFILE
PM               ONLINE_MEDIA          PRODUCT_AUDIO              ORDAUDIO
PM               PRINT_MEDIA           AD_HEADER                  ADHEADER_TYP
PM               ONLINE_MEDIA          PRODUCT_PHOTO_SIGNATURE    ORDIMAGESIGNATURE
PM               ONLINE_MEDIA          PRODUCT_PHOTO              ORDIMAGE
PM               ONLINE_MEDIA          PRODUCT_TESTIMONIALS       ORDDOC
SH               MVIEW$_EXCEPTIONS     BAD_ROWID                  ROWID

19 rows selected.
```

2. Ensure the identifiers line uniqueness
   We query DB_LOGSTANDBY_NOT_UNIQUE view

3. As for the physical standby database, we ensure that the primary database is in ARCHIVELOG mode and that mode FORCE LOGGING is activated.

4. Enable additional logging

☞ If you create the standby database by Enterprise Manager, the activation is done automatically and in manual mode, you do so by:

```
SQL> ALTER DATABASE ADD Supplemental LOG DATA
(PRIMARY KEY, UNIQUE INDEX) COLUMNS;
```

The columns SUPPLEMENTAL _LOG_DATA_MIN, SUPPLEMENTAL_ LOG _DATA_ PK and SUPPLEMENTAL _ LOG_DATA_UI of the view V$database take value YES.

In the following steps, we will convert the physical standby database (stdbyl1) previously created in a logical standby database.

5. Stop LOG APPLY on the physical standby database.

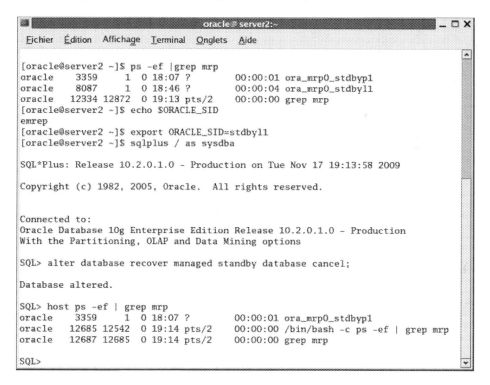

This in order to not apply the subsequent changes to redo log containing the dictionary log miner.

☞ **Caution**: Do not use the clause FINISH instead of CANCEL, as this will result in the permanent cessation of REDO LOG APPLY on the standby database and the latter can be opened only in READ ONLY mode or be converted into a primary database.

6. Prepare the primary database to support a logical standby database.

   6-a Setting of LOG_ARCHIVE_DEST _n
   6-b Assignment of 3600 to UNDO_RETENTION for improving building log miner dictionary performance.

```
SQL> ALTER SYSTEM SET UNDO_RETENTION = 3600;
```

7. Build a log miner dictionary in the redo logs.
It is recommended to build the dictionary outside the SYSAUX tablespace which is the default location for performance reasons.

```
SQL> create tablespace logmnr_tbs datafile
'/u01/app/oracle/oradata/orcl/lgmnr_tbs01.dbf'
2> size 20M autoextend on;
Tablespace created.
SQL>exec dbms_logmnr_d.set_tablespace('logmnr_tbs')
SQL > EXEC DBMS_LOGSTDBY.BUILD ;
```

8. Make the transition to the logical database

   8-a) Change the physical database to logical database.

```
SQL>ALTER   DATABASE   RECOVER   TO   LOGICAL   STANDBY
stdbyl1;
```

This command changes the name of the database that was orcl to stdbyl1 in the control file and automatically updates the SPFILE.

We check that the database is changed to the logical type by referring to the field
DATABASE_ROLE in the V$DATABASE view.

```
SQL>SELECT DATABASE_ROLE FROM V$DATABASE;
Return LOGICAL STANDBY
```

8-b) Create a new password file (to support the new name of the database.)

$ orapwd file = $ORACLE_HOME/dbs/orapwstdbyl1 pasword=oracle force = y

8-c) Stop and restart the database in MOUNT

```
SQL> SHUTDOWN IMMEDIATE;
SQL> STATUP MOUNT
```

9. Open the logical standby database and start the SQL apply service

```
a) SQL> alter database open RESETLOGS;
b) SQL> Alter database start logical standby [apply
immediate];
```

The IMMEDIATE clause allows the application of the SQL issued from the logs received in real time, requires the presence of standby redo logfiles.

```
oracle@ server2:/u01/app/oracle/product/10.2.0/db_1/dbs          _ □ ✕
Fichier  Édition  Affichage  Terminal  Onglets  Aide

SQL*Plus: Release 10.2.0.1.0 - Production on Tue Nov 17 20:07:42 2009

Copyright (c) 1982, 2005, Oracle.  All rights reserved.


Connected to:
Oracle Database 10g Enterprise Edition Release 10.2.0.1.0 - Production
With the Partitioning, OLAP and Data Mining options

SQL> alter database open resetlogs;

Database altered.

SQL> alter database start logical standby apply;

Database altered.

SQL> host ps -ef |grep lsp
oracle    26742      1  2 20:40 ?        00:00:00 ora_lsp0_stdbyl1
oracle    26812 20618  0 20:41 pts/3     00:00:00 /bin/bash -c ps -ef |grep lsp
oracle    26814 26812  0 20:41 pts/3     00:00:00 grep lsp

SQL>
```

10. Check the proper functioning of the logical standby database
We consult the following views:

`V$LOGSTANDBY_PROGRESS`

Contains information about the progress of SQL APPLY

APPLIED_SCN: larger Scn applied.
LATEST_SCN: SCN received (last) but not yet applied
RESTART_SCN: latest number of SCN where APPLY started
MINING_SCN: latest number of SCN treated by the process Builder

`V$LOGSTANDBY_STATE`

Contains information on the status of the logical standby process:

SESSION_ ID: Id of the session log miner allocated to SQL Apply
REALTIME_APPLY indicates whether yes (Y) or no (N) applying is in real time.
STATE: state of a process allocated to SQL APPLY, may take the following values:
INITIALIZING: in progress (session log miner has been created)
LOADING DICTIONARY: Dictionary log miner is being loaded by SQL Apply
WAITING ON GAP: SQL Apply is waiting for a log file from the primary data tabase
APPLYING: transactions are being applied
IDLE: all logs received have been applied (by SQL apply) and the latter is at rest
WAITING FOR DICTIONARY LOGS: The archive log containing the log miner dictionary has not yet been received from the primary database and SQL Apply is waiting for it.

`V$LOGSTANDBY_STATS`

Contains the Log Miner statistics and information on the status of log standby during SQL apply:

```
NAME: statistic name
Value: value of the statistic
Some values for Name are :
Number of preparers, Number of appliers,
Coordinator State, Transactions applied, Transactions
scheduled, Transactions skipped.
Number of DDL Applied, Number of DDL Transactions
skipped
```

```
DBA_LOGSTDBY_LOG
```

Contains information on the logs stored in the logical standby database.

FILENAME: file name
SEQUENCE #: log sequence number
DICT_BEGIN (YES, NO), means whether or not the beginning of the dictionary is included
in this archive
DICT_END (YES, NO) means whether or not the end of the dictionary is included
APPLIED (YES, NO, CURRENT)
FIRST_CHANGE# SCN of the current archive log
NEXT_CHANGE# SCN of the next archive log

```
V$LOGSTANDBY_PROCESS
```

Provides information on the current state of SQL Apply process.

SID
Serial ≠ } unique identifier for the session

SID ⟷ SPID of the view V$process

TYPE: type of treatment going on (coordinator, Reader, Builder, Prepare, Analyzer, Applier)
HIGH_SCN: bigger SCN treated by this process

Caution

If the view Dba_logstdby_log returns no row or column STATE of the view V$logstandby_state returns "waiting for dictionnary LOGS", it means that the archived logs on the primary database from when the dictionary log miner was built have not yet been registered on the standby database.
If so, proceed as follows:
Stop first the SQL Apply and then:

a) Find the log in the primary database by :

```
colum name format a60
Select name,dest_id,sequence# from v$archived_log
where (sequence#= (select max(sequence#) from
v$archived_log where DICTIONARY_BEGIN = 'YES' and
standby_dest='NO'));
```

b) Copy this log file archive (one on choice) on the standby database and, register by :

```
SQL> ALTER DATABASE REGISTER LOGFILE '/path/file' ;
```
Restart the SQL Apply

Make a log switch on the primary database and make sure that the log is received and applied (SQL apply) on the standby database.

```
oracle@server2:/u01/app/oracle/product/10.2.0/db_1/admin/orcl/bdump

Fichier  Édition  Affichage  Terminal  Onglets  Aide
SQL> select sequence#,dict_begin,dict_end,applied from dba_logstdby_log;

SEQUENCE# DIC DIC APPLIED
---------- --- --- --------
        73 NO  NO  CURRENT

SQL> /

SEQUENCE# DIC DIC APPLIED
---------- --- --- --------
        73 NO  NO  CURRENT

SQL> select applied_scn,newest_scn from dba_logstdby_progress;

APPLIED_SCN NEWEST_SCN
----------- ----------
     819150     821120

SQL> select sequence#,dict_begin,dict_end,applied from dba_logstdby_log;

SEQUENCE# DIC DIC APPLIED
---------- --- --- --------
        73 NO  NO  CURRENT

SQL> /

SEQUENCE# DIC DIC APPLIED
---------- --- --- --------
        74 NO  NO  CURRENT

SQL>
```

Caution

After converting the physical standby database to the logical standby database with SQL, the status of that database will appear in error in Enterprise Manager (as shown below). You must delete it from the Data Guard Broker, then add it again to obtain a correct status without error.

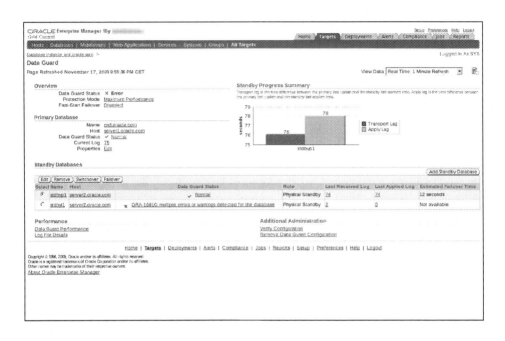

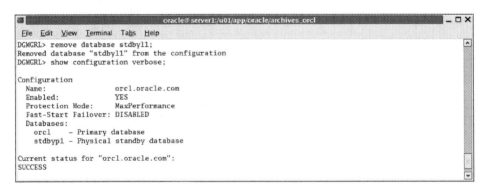

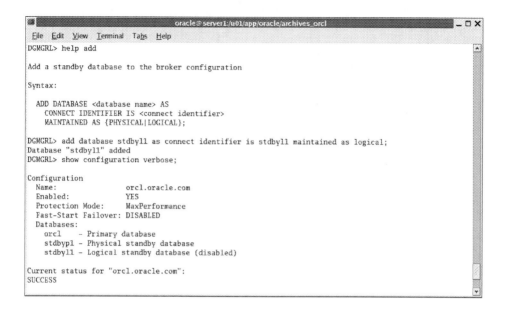

```
oracle@server1:/u01/app/oracle/archives_orcl                     _ □ ×
File  Edit  View  Terminal  Tabs  Help
DGMGRL> help add

Add a standby database to the broker configuration

Syntax:

  ADD DATABASE <database name> AS
    CONNECT IDENTIFIER IS <connect identifier>
    MAINTAINED AS {PHYSICAL|LOGICAL};

DGMGRL> add database stdbyl1 as connect identifier is stdbyl1 maintained as logical;
Database "stdbyl1" added
DGMGRL> show configuration verbose;

Configuration
  Name:                orcl.oracle.com
  Enabled:             YES
  Protection Mode:     MaxPerformance
  Fast-Start Failover: DISABLED
  Databases:
    orcl    - Primary database
    stdbyp1 - Physical standby database
    stdbyl1 - Logical standby database (disabled)

Current status for "orcl.oracle.com":
SUCCESS
```

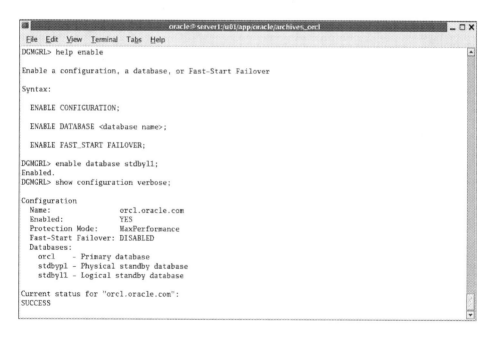

```
oracle@server1:/u01/app/oracle/archives_orcl                     _ □ ×
File  Edit  View  Terminal  Tabs  Help
DGMGRL> help enable

Enable a configuration, a database, or Fast-Start Failover

Syntax:

  ENABLE CONFIGURATION;

  ENABLE DATABASE <database name>;

  ENABLE FAST_START FAILOVER;

DGMGRL> enable database stdbyl1;
Enabled.
DGMGRL> show configuration verbose;

Configuration
  Name:                orcl.oracle.com
  Enabled:             YES
  Protection Mode:     MaxPerformance
  Fast-Start Failover: DISABLED
  Databases:
    orcl    - Primary database
    stdbyp1 - Physical standby database
    stdbyl1 - Logical standby database

Current status for "orcl.oracle.com":
SUCCESS
```

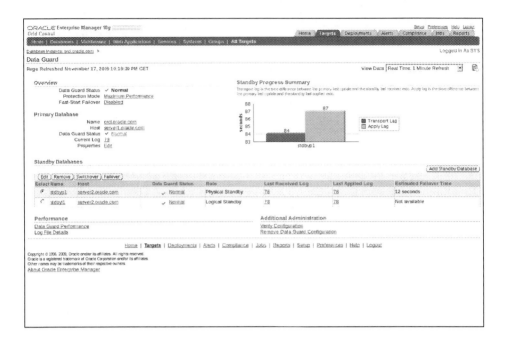

Note: Since version 10g R2, archived redo logs are auto deleted by SQL Apply on the logical database standby (but kept on the primary database). To preserve them, run on the standby database the command:
SQL> exec DBMS_LOGSTDBY.APPLY_SET ('LOG_AUTO_DELETE','FALSE');

CHAPTER 8

DATA PROTECTION METHODS &
REDO LOG TRANSFER SERVICES

Data Guard provides three types of data protection:

- MAXIMUM PERFORMANCE
- MAXIMUM AVAILABILITY
- MAXIMUM PROTECTION.

MAXIMUM PROTECTION

This protection mode offers a total guarantee against data loss. No difference between the production site and standby site is tolerated. To do this, the primary database automatically stops if an error prevents it from writing generated redo log information on the primary database to at least one standby site.

MAXIMUM AVAILABILITY

This mode as the previous offers a full guarantee against data loss, but unlike the latter, the primary database is not stopped if the redo log files information cannot be written to at least one standby location. A temporary difference is allowed between the production site and standby until such time as the shift logs not received on the STANDBY be actually written. On the otherhand, we may have data loss if a second problem occurred preventing the primary database to send redo log information to at least one standby database.

MAXIMUM PERFORMANCE

This is the default protection mode. In this mode, transactions are validated (or considered as such), when the associated redo log information have been written in the redo log file of the primary database. The primary database is not stopped if the information redo log files have not been written on any standby site. There may be loss of data in this mode.

STANDBY REDO LOGFILES

These are log files of a particular type used only on standby database. However, it is recommended to create them also on the primary base to facilitate the role change.
These files are required in the following cases:

- Level of protection other than maximal performance.
- Redo log Apply in real time
- Destination of Redo logfile in cascade.

The number of standby Redo logfiles must be at least strictly greater than the number of standard redo logfiles and larger than the maximum size of standard Redo log.

WHAT PROTECTION MODE SELECT?

The choice is made according to operational constraints. The maximum protection mode should be adopted with caution due to inadvertent disruption of the primary database in case of transfer failure and / or logs write issue to the standby sites (e.g. network failure). If you must use this mode, it is strongly recommended to have at least two standby databases in the data guard configuration

CONFIGURATION OF PROTECTION MODES

The configuration is done in two steps:

- Defining the type of transfer redo logs information to standby sites
- Application of the protection mode on the primary database.

1) Defining the type of transfer:

For protection methods other than maximum performance, transmitting redo logfiles information must be made synchronously with the process LOG writer. We have seen above that in this case, there must be at least n+1 standby log on the standby database (where n is the number of standard redo log files on the primary database). The clause AFFIRM must also be specified in the parameter LOG_ARCHIVE_DEST_n, This clause ensures that redo log informations sent were well written to disk on the standby site (it is sort of a receipt). For maximum performance mode, sending redo log information can be made a asynchronously (by the LGWR process, in this case we specify LGWR ASYNC or by the archiving process in which case we specify ASYNC)

```
Example  of  value  for  LOG_ARCHIVE_DEST_n  in  the
initialization parameters file
Log_archive_dest_n ='service = stdby11
LGWR ASYNC NOAFFIRM db_unique_name = "stdby11 "'.
```

☞ **NB** :In Data Guard broker configuration, the modification of parameters LOG_ARCHIVE_DEST_n should not be done with the command **SQL ALTER SYSTEM** because it may cause a status error in the broker. Instead, use in this case the command EDIT DATABASE of DGMGRL.

2) Application of the protection method on the primary database

It can be done either in SQL or with the command DGMGRL or with Enterprise Manager

a) Using SQL

```
SQL> ALTER DATABASE SET STANDBY DATABASE TO
MAXIMIZE { PROTECTION | AVAILABILITY | PERFORMANCE}
```

This command is to be performed on the primary database, the database being in MOUNT mode.

At the end of the execution of this command, the database automatically restarts.

b) With orders DGMGRL

```
DGMGRL> EDIT CONFIGURATION SET PROTECTION MODE
AS {MAXAVAILIABILITY | MAX PERFORMANCE |
MAXPROTECTION}
```

Caution: An attempt to perform this command while the primary database orcl is not registered statically as shown in chapter 5, will generate an error at the end of the process.

```
oracle@server1:~                                                    _ □ ✕
File  Edit  View  Terminal  Tabs  Help
[oracle@server1 ~]$ dgmgrl
DGMGRL for Linux: Version 10.2.0.1.0 - Production

Copyright (c) 2000, 2005, Oracle. All rights reserved.

Welcome to DGMGRL, type "help" for information.
DGMGRL> connect sys/oracle
Connected.
DGMGRL> edit database 'stdbyp1' set property 'LogXptMode'='SYNC';
Property "LogXptMode" updated
DGMGRL> edit database 'stdbyl1' set property 'LogXptMode'='SYNC';
Property "LogXptMode" updated
DGMGRL> edit configuration set protection mode as maxavailability;
Operation requires shutdown of instance "orcl" on database "orcl"
Shutting down instance "orcl"...
Database closed.
Database dismounted.
ORACLE instance shut down.
Operation requires startup of instance "orcl" on database "orcl"
Starting instance "orcl"...
Unable to connect to database
ORA-12514: TNS:listener does not currently know of service requested in connect descriptor

Failed.
You are no longer connected to ORACLE
Please connect again.
Unable to start instance "orcl"
You must start instance "orcl" manually
DGMGRL> █
```

Let us proceed to this registration and perform the command again.

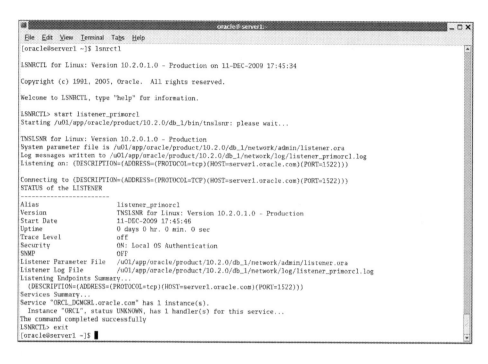

It is now successful.

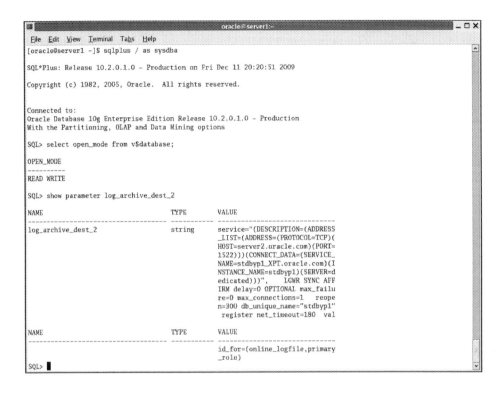

We check the value of Log_archive_2 in SQL

Caution:

- The Edit database command must also be performed on at least one standby site.
- The application of data protection mode with DGMGRL is made on primary at opened state, this order involves stopping the database, the start of the instance to the state Mount and the effective implementation of protection mode
- Although at the end of this command, the status of the database displayed in DGMGRL is mounted, effective status of the primary database is OPEN READ-WRITE as displayed in SQL.

- The instance of the primary database must be properly registered with the listener statically as seen in chapter 5 if not, automatic restart will be impossible.
- When registering, be careful to the SID case, if you use the operating system LINUX / UNIX

You can check through the command Show parameter LOG_ARCHIVE_DEST_n that the modification of type of service of redo log transfer made by DGMGRL have fully updated the file SPFILE.

A change of this parameter by the **SQL> ALTER SYSTEM** would not involve any change in DGMGRL, worse, it would have caused an error status of Data Guard.

c) WITH ENTERPRISE MANAGER

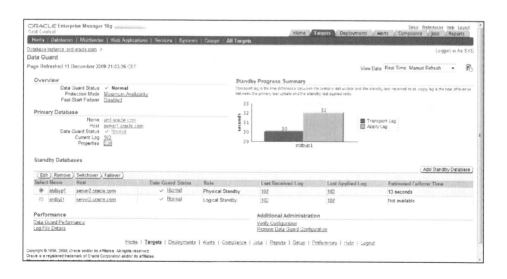

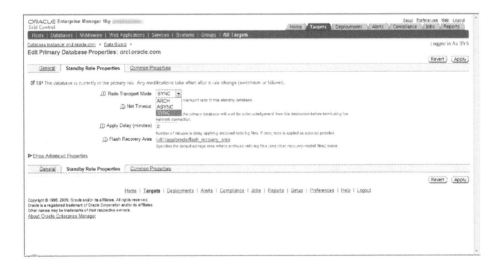

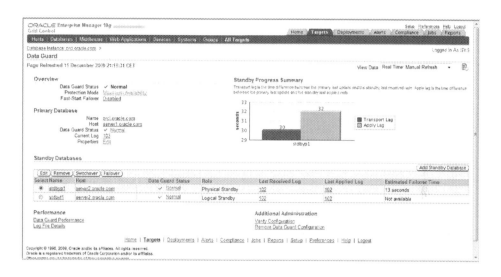

☞ In Enterprise Manager, at the section protection mode, we have the choice between ARCH, ASYNC and SNYC, behold their equivalents with the terms of the parameter LOG_ARCHIVE_DEST_n

ENTERPRISE MANAGER	SQL
ARCH	ARCH
ASYNC	LGWR ASYNC NOAFFIRM
SYNC	LGWR SYNC AFFIRM

## CHAPTER 9

ROLES SWITCHOVER &
BASE CHANGE (FAILOVER)

A database in a Data Guard can have two types of roles:

- Primary database role
- Standby database (physical or logical) role.

The type of role can be obtained from the DATABASE_ROLE column in the V$database view.

Services management of roles in a Data Guard configuration allow switchover of roles (SWITCHOVER) or change of the base in case of failure of the primary database (FAILOVER)

SWITCHOVER OF ROLES

The switchover is used as part of planned maintenance interventions on the hardware or operating system. At the successful completion of the operation, the old standby database becomes the primary base and vice versa. The contents of the new primary database are identical to the old database. Thus, a permutation should never be used to solve a problem of incomplete recovery.

Scenario

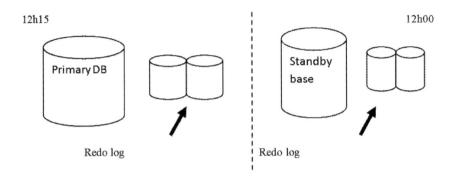

12h15   12h00

Primary DB   Standby base

Redo log   Redo log

Committed transactions on the primary data base at 12 h 15

Transactions applied on the standby database at 12h. No flashback database enabled on the databases.
Validated data since 12 h on the primary base is incorrect.

QUESTION: Will the permutation of the roles of the two databases bring back the new primary base in its state at 12h.

No, because at the (successful) end of the switchover, the new primary database will contain all committed transactions after 12 h.

FAILOVER

To be performed in case of emergency.

Example: The primary database is down or corrupted and you feel that recovery is impossible or will take a long time.
Unlike the permutation of roles, there may be data loss by way of data protection applied.
Since version 10g R2, it is possible to make an automatic database change, by enabling FAST START FAILOVER functionality which will be discussed in the next chapter.

SWITCHOVER OF ROLES

It must be made on the primary database.
If the permutation concerns a physical database standby, the two databases are restarted, however the other standby database do not need to be restarted.

If the switchover concerns a logical standby database, it is not necessary to restart any database.
Roles Switchover, like the Failover can be done in three ways:

- By Enterprise Manager
- By DGMGRL
- By SQL

We will describe below some of these methods

A) SWITCHOVER OF ROLES WITH A PHYSICAL standby database USING SQL COMMANDS.

a) In the original primary database instance

1 - Check that the permutation is possible. By accessing the field SWITCHOVER_STATUS of the V$database view. It must contain "TO STANDBY" or "SESSIONS ACTIVE".

2 - Change the role of the primary database (by passing it to the standby role) by the command:

```
SQL> Alter database COMMIT TO SWITCHOVER TO PHYSICAL
STANDBY [WITH SESSION SHUTDOWN];
```

The session clause is required if the sessions are active, otherwise an error is generated.

3 - Shutdown and restart the instance in MOUNT mode:

```
SQL> SHUTDOWN IMMEDIATE;
SQL> STARTUP MOUNT;
```

b) In the original physical standby database instance.

1. Verify that the change of role can be done by querying in the column SWITCHOVER_STATUS of the V$database view. It must contain 'TO PRIMARY' or 'SESSIONS ACTIVE' if neither of these values is returned that means that Redo Apply is not ACTIVE. Check and start it

2. Change the role of the database by the command.

```
SQL> ALTER DATABASE COMMIT TO SWITCHOVER TO PRIMARY
[WITH SESSION SHUTDOWN];
```

3. If the database is opened in read only mode, restart the instance and open the database (new primary database) in Read/Write mode; If it is mounted set it in Read/Write mode.

4. At this stage, the old standby database has become the primary base, the location of archive logs must be specified (if not already done by assigning appropriate values to the parameters LOG_ARCHIVE_DEST_n.)
   The test of sending information of generated redo log files on the primary database (new) is made by the command.

```
SQL> ALTER SYSTEM SWITCH LOGFILE;
```
and checking its reception and application on the new standby database by querying the V$MANEGED_STANDBY view;

The start of log apply is only necessary if this service was stopped. In this case do

```
SQL> ALTER DATABASE RECOVER MANAGED STANDBY DATABASE
[USING CURRENT LOGFILE] DISCONNECT FROM SESSIONS;
```

☞ If the Data Guard configuration contains a logical standby database, on the old physical standby database which became the primary, enable the additional logging with the command.

```
SQL> ALTER DATABASE ADD SUPPLEMENTAL LOG DATA
(PRIMAIRY KEY, UNIQUE INDEX) COLUMNS;
```

B-SWITCHOVER WITH A LOGICAL STANDBY database by SQL COMMANDS

a) In the original primary database
1 - Column SWITCHOVER_STATUS of the V$database view must contain "TO STANDBY" OR "SESSIONS ACTIVE"
2 - Prepare the database to be a logical standby database.

```
SQL> ALTER DATABASE PREPARE TO SWITCHOVER TO LOGICAL
STANDBY;
```

b) In the initial logical standby database
- Prepare the database to become the primary base with the command

```
SQL> ALTER DATABASE PREPARE TO SWITCHOVER TO PRIMARY;
```

After that command, the column SWITCHOVER_STATUS of V$DATABASE will show PREPARING DICTIONARY

At this moment the standby sites receive the redo logs but do not apply them yet.

c) In the original primary database.
1 - Check that the column SWITCHOVER_STATUS of the V$database view contains
"TO LOGICAL STANDBY".

2 - Change the role of the database to logical standby database:

```
SQL> ALTER DATABASE COMMIT TO SWITCHOVER TO LOGICAL
STANDBY;
```
This command waits the end of all pending transactions before executing. It prevents users from changing data maintained in the standby database.

It is recommended to close the sessions on the primary database before performing this command for performance reasons.

d) In the new primary database

1 - Check that the column SWITCHOVER_STATUS of the V$database view contains "TO PRIMARY"

2 - Change the role of the primary database:

```
SQL> ALTER DATABASE COMMIT TO SWITCHOVER TO PRIMARY;
```

e) In the new logical standby database, start SQL Apply

```
SQL> ALTER DATABASE START LOGICAL STANDBY APPLY
[IMMEDIATE];
```

FAILOVER

The former primary database is no longer part of the Data Guard configuration after change.

The former primary database can be reinstated as standby database (by the command REINSTATE), for this, flashback database should have been enabled and sufficient flashback logs produced.

There is also a possibility to activate a standby database (to transform it into a primary database).

☞ If a failover is performed on a logical standby database, all other logical standby databases are permanently disabled and become unusable.

C-FAILOVER WITH A PHYSICAL STANDBY database BY THE SQL COMMANDS

1) Identify and correct the gaps between redo archives of the two sites.

We consult the viewV$ARCHIVE_GAP of the physical standby database. It must be empty. If not, identify the missing archives (by consulting the view V$archived_log) on the standby database, copy them from the primary database and register them on the physical standby database:

SQL> ALTER DATABASE REGISTER PHYSICAL LOGFILE 'Path /file';

If the protection mode of the database is MAXIMUM PROTECTION, there should not be offset of logs archive between the two sites, this first step can be ignored in this case.

Repeat this step until V$ARCHIVE_GAP contains no rows.

☞ If the primary database can be put into MOUNT mode, the generated archives on the primary not yet applied to the physical standby database can be made in a single order in 11g version:

SQL> ALTER SYSTEM FLUSH REDO TO db_unique_stdbyname;

the db _unique_stdbyname is the db _unique_name of the physical standby database where you want to register the missing logs.

2) Stop definitively the Apply logs on the standby database.

SQL> ALTER DATABASE RECOVER MANAGED STANDBY DATABASE FINISH FORCE;

3) Convert the physical standby database as primary database:

ₙSQL> ALTER DATABASE COMMIT TO SWITCHOVER TO PRIMARY [WITH SESSION SHUTDOWN];

4) Open the database by

SQL> Alter database OPEN; (if in MOUNT mode) or
SQL> Shutdown immediate;
SQL> startup;
If it was previously opened.

5) Perform the backup of the database by RMAN (step not required but strongly recommended)

D—FAILOVER WITH A LOGICAL STANDBY DATABASE USING SQL COMMANDS.

1 - Copy the missing log files to the logical standby database and register them as for the physical standby database

```
SQL> ALTER DATABASE REGISTER LOGICAL LOGFILE '/path/ file';
```

☞ Here we can't query the V$archive_gap view because it is always empty for a logical standby database.

If you use 11g version of the database and the primary database can be put into MOUNT mode, proceed as seen on previous page to copy the missing logs and apply the command

```
SQL> ALTER SYSTEM FLUSH REDO ...
```

2 - Check the DBA_LOGSTDBY_PROGRESS view to ensure that all logs received have been applied. This occurs if the values of the column APPLIED_SCN and LATEST_SCN are equal.

3 - Activate the new primary database:

```
SQL> ALTER DATABASE ACTIVATE LOGICAL STANDBY DATABASE
FINISH APPLY;
```

4 - On all other Logical standby databas of theData Guard configuration:

- Create a database link that is pointing to the primary database (public link with the user system)
- Start SQL Apply.

```
SQL> ALTER DATABASE START LOGICAL STANDBY APPLY NEW
PRIMARY dblink;
All other logical standby databases in advance on the
new primary database must be recreated.
Other methods of switch-over roles and FAILOVER will
be discussed at the work practices of this chapter.
```

EXERCISES

-1 Enable flashback database on the primary database and the two standby databases with a retention period of 24 hours.

Enabling flashback database can be done either through Enterprise Manager or by SQL commands. For physical standby, database in MOUNT state, we activate by SQL commands.

```
oracle@server2:~                                    _ □ ×
File  Edit  View  Terminal  Tabs  Help
[oracle@server2 ~]$ export ORACLE_SID=stdbyp1
[oracle@server2 ~]$ sqlplus / as sysdba

SQL*Plus: Release 10.2.0.1.0 - Production on Mon Dec 14 20:26:35 2009

Copyright (c) 1982, 2005, Oracle.  All rights reserved.


Connected to:
Oracle Database 10g Enterprise Edition Release 10.2.0.1.0 - Production
With the Partitioning, OLAP and Data Mining options

SQL> set sqlprompt 'PHY>'
PHY>alter database recover managed standby database cancel;

Database altered.

PHY>alter database flashback on;

Database altered.

PHY>alter system set db_flashback_retention_target=1440;

System altered.

PHY>shutdown immediate;
ORA-01109: database not open


Database dismounted.
ORACLE instance shut down.
PHY>startup mount;
ORACLE instance started.

Total System Global Area  536870912 bytes
Fixed Size                  1220432 bytes
Variable Size             150995120 bytes
Database Buffers          381681664 bytes
Redo Buffers                2973696 bytes
Database mounted.
PHY>█
```

For the primary database and logical standby database, we proceed by the Enterprise Manager console.

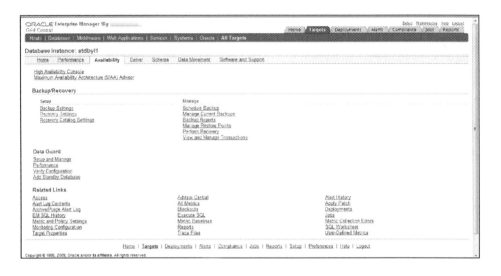

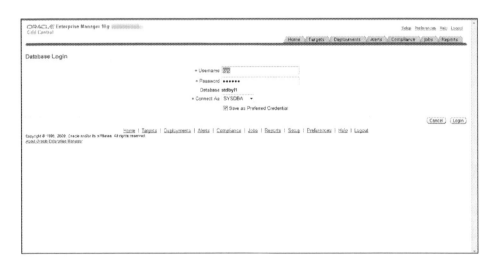

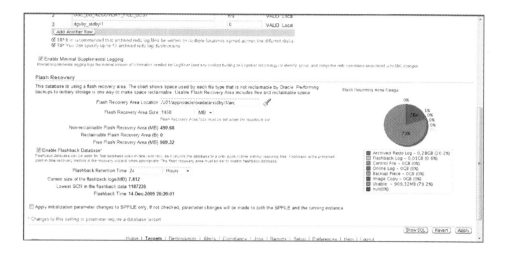

After you click on Apply, the instance restarts

2 - Set the parameter Net_TIMEOUT to 1 minute and the parameter
    LOG_archive_trace to 130 = 128 +2.

This value allows us to track the status of archiving files redolog (2) and
the activity of the process FAL (128)

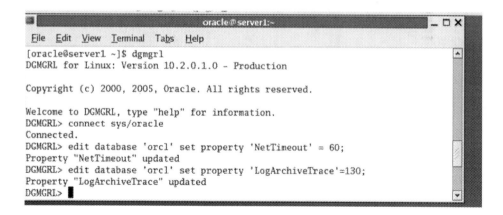

3 - Clear destinations archive number 2 and number 3 or disconnect
    the network connection to server 2.

Log on the primary database with the user hr et run following command:

SQL> update set employee last_name = 'Test **' | | 'last-name;

SQL> commit ; / * note the time of the commit */

SQL > conn / as sysdba

SQL> Alter system switch logfile;

Reestablish communication or re-enable archiving destinations. Check the log files and comment.

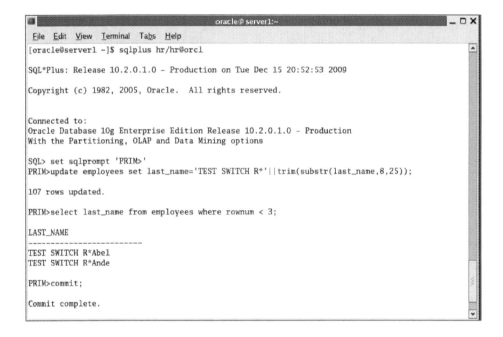

We display the last 50 lines of file alert

$ cd /u01/app/oracle/admin/oracl/bdump

$ tail—50 alert-orcl.log

```
Destination LOG_ARCHIVE_DEST_2 IS SYNCHRONIZED
LGWR: Standby redo logfile selected to archive
thread 1 sequence 137
LGWR: Standby redo logfile selected for thread 1
sequence 137 for destination LOG_ARCHIVE_DEST_3
```

LGWR: Standby redo logfile selected to archive thread 1 sequence 137 LGWR: Standby redo logfile selected for thread 1 sequence 137 for destination LOG_ARCHIVE_DEST_2 Thread 1 advanced to log sequence 137 Current log # 1 seq # 137 mem # 0: / u01/app/oracle/oradata/orcl/redo01.log
Mon December 14 2009 9:15:08 p.m.
ALTER SYSTEM SET log_archive_trace = 130 SCOPE = BOTH SID = 'orcl';
My December 14 2009 9:31:13 p.m.
ORA-16198: LGWR timedout Received error from KSR
LGWR: Attempting destination LOG_ARCHIVE_DEST_2 network reconnect (16198)
LGWR: Destination network reconnect LOG_ARCHIVE_DEST_2 abandoned
Mon December 14 2009 9:31:13 p.m.
Errors in file / u01/app/oracle/admin/orcl/bdump/orcl_lgwr_10324.trc:
ORA-16198: Timeout incurred on internal channel DURING remote archival
LGWR: Network asynch I / O wait error log 16,198 a Service '(DESCRIPTION = (ADDRESS_LIST = (ADDRESS = (PROTOCOL = TCP) (HOST = server2.oracle.com) (PORT = 1522))) (CONNECT_DATA = (SERVICE_NAME = stdbyp1_XPT.oracle.com) (instance_name = stdbyp1) (SERVER = Dedicated)))'
My December 14 2009 9:31:13 p.m.
Destination LOG_ARCHIVE_DEST_2 IS unsynchronized
ORA-16198: LGWR timedout Received error from KSR
LGWR: Attempting destination LOG_ARCHIVE_DEST_3 network reconnect (16198)
LGWR: Destination LOG_ARCHIVE_DEST_3 networks reconnect abandoned
Mon December 14 2009 9:31:13 p.m.
Errors in file / u01/app/oracle/admin/orcl/bdump/orcl_lgwr_10324.trc:
ORA-16198: Timeout incurred on internal channel DURING remote archival

LGWR: Network asynch I / O wait error log 16,198 a Service
'(DESCRIPTION = (ADDRESS_LIST = (ADDRESS = (PROTOCOL =
TCP) (HOST = server2.oracle.com) (PORT = 1523)))
(CONNECT_DATA = (SERVICE_NAME = stdbyl1_XPT.oracle.com)
(instance_name = stdbyl1) (SERVER = Dedicated)))'
Mon December 14 2009 9:31:13 p.m.
Destination LOG_ARCHIVE_DEST_3 IS unsynchronized
LGWR: Failed to archive log 1 thread 1 sequence 137
(16198) Mon. December 14 2009 9:31:13 p.m.
LGWR: Closing remote archive destination LOG_ARCHIVE_
DEST_2: '(DESCRIPTION = (ADDRESS_LIST = (ADDRESS =
(PROTOCOL = TCP) (HOST = server2.oracle.com) (PORT =
1522))) (CONNECT_DATA = (SERVICE_NAME = stdbyp1_XPT.
oracle.com) (instance_name = stdbyp1) (SERVER =
Dedicated))) '(error 16198)
(Orcl) Mon. December 14 2009 9:31:13 p.m. Errors in file
/ u01/app/oracle/admin/orcl/bdump/orcl_lgwr_10324.trc:
**ORA-16198: Timeout incurred on internal channel DURING
remote archival LGWR: Error 16198 closing archivelog file
'(DESCRIPTION = (ADDRESS_LIST = (ADDRESS = (PROTOCOL = TCP)
(HOST = server2.oracle.com) (PORT = 1522))) (CONNECT_DATA
= (SERVICE_NAME = stdbyp1_XPT.oracle.com) (instance_name
= stdbyp1) (SERVER = Dedicated)))'**
Mon December 14 2009 9:31:13 p.m.
**LGWR: Closing remote archive destination LOG_ARCHIVE_DEST_3:
'(DESCRIPTION = (ADDRESS_LIST = (ADDRESS = (PROTOCOL = TCP)
(HOST = server2.oracle.com) (PORT = 1523))) (CONNECT_DATA
= (SERVICE_NAME = stdbyl1_XPT.oracle.com) (instance_name
= stdbyl1) (SERVER = Dedicated))) '(error 16198)(Orcl)**
Mon December 14 2009 9:31:13 p.m.
Errors in file / u01/app/oracle/admin/orcl/bdump/orcl_
lgwr_10324.trc:
ORA-16198: Timeout incurred on internal channel
DURING remote archival
LGWR: Error 16198 closing archivelog file
'(DESCRIPTION = (ADDRESS_LIST = (ADDRESS = (PROTOCOL
= TCP) (HOST = server2.oracle.com) (PORT = 1523)))

(CONNECT_DATA = (SERVICE_NAME = stdbyl1_XPT.oracle.
com) (instance_name = stdbyl1) (SERVER = Dedicated)))'
LGWR: Error 16198 disconnecting from destination
LOG_ARCHIVE_DEST_2 standby host '(DESCRIPTION =
(ADDRESS_LIST = (ADDRESS = (PROTOCOL = TCP) (HOST =
server2.oracle.com) (PORT = 1522))) (CONNECT_DATA =
(SERVICE_NAME = stdbyp1_XPT.oracle.com) (instance_name
= stdbyp1) (SERVER = Dedicated))) 'Mon December 14 2009
9:31:23 p.m. LGWR: Error 16198 disconnecting
from destination LOG_ARCHIVE_DEST_3 standby
host '(DESCRIPTION = (ADDRESS_LIST = (ADDRESS =
(PROTOCOL = TCP) (HOST = server2.oracle.com) (PORT
= 1523))) (CONNECT_DATA = (SERVICE_NAME = stdbyl1_
XPT.oracle.com) (instance_name = stdbyl1) (SERVER =
Dedicated)))'
Thread 1 advanced to log sequence 138 Current log
2 seq # 138 mem # 0:u01/app/oracle/oradata/orcl/
redo02.log
Mon December 14 9:34:46 p.m. in 2009
**Thread 1 advanced to log sequence 139 Current log #
3 seq # 139 mem # 0: /**
u01/app/oracle/oradata/orcl/redo03.log Mon December
14 2009 9:44:41 p.m.

ARC0: Attempting destination LOG_ARCHIVE_DEST_3 network
reconnect (3113) ARC0: Destination network reconnect LOG_
ARCHIVE_DEST_3 abandonné PING [ARC0]: Error 3113

When pinging standby (DESCRIPTION = (ADDRESS_LIST =
(ADDRESS = (PROTOCOL = TCP) (HOST Server2.oracle.
com =) (PORT = 1523)))
(CONNECT_DATA = (SERVICE_NAME = stdbyl1_XPT.oracle.
com) (instance name = stdbyl1) (SERVER = Dedicated))).
Mon December 14 2009 10:00:22 p.m.
ARC0: Attempting destination LOG_ARCHIVE_DEST_2
network reconnect (3113)
ARC0: Destination network LOG_ARCHIVE_DEST_2
Reconnects abandoned

PING [ARC0]: Error 3113 When pinging standby

Writing errors logs are filled in this extract. The current log is at 139, and the last log received on the two standby database is number 136, thus gap.

We can also see in this gap in the Data Guard Page in Enterprise Manager which follows.

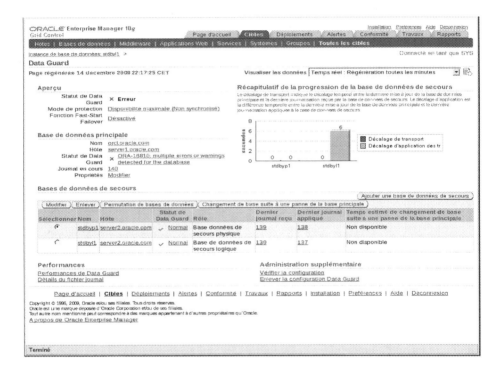

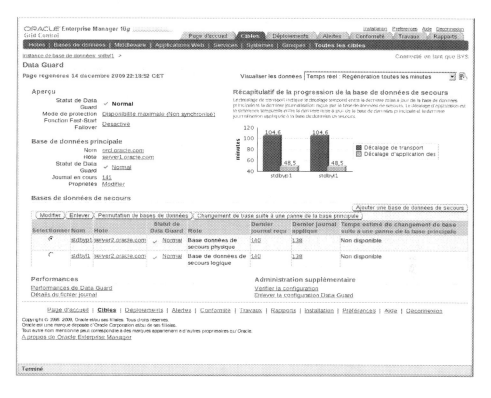

We see that after the restoration of the network connection, the logs that were not sent are progressively transmitted and applied on the two standby databases (by redo apply on the physical and on the logical by SQL Apply).

Check on the logical standby database if changes on the names have been applied.

```
                            oracle@ server1:~                        _ □ ×
File   Edit   View   Terminal   Tabs   Help
[oracle@server1 ~]$ sqlplus hr/hr@stdby11

SQL*Plus: Release 10.2.0.1.0 - Production on Mon Dec 14 22:24:29 2009

Copyright (c) 1982, 2005, Oracle.  All rights reserved.


Connected to:
Oracle Database 10g Enterprise Edition Release 10.2.0.1.0 - Production
With the Partitioning, OLAP and Data Mining options

SQL> select last_name from employees where rownum < 20;

LAST_NAME
---------------------------------------
TEST **Abel
TEST **Ande
TEST **Atkinson
TEST **Austin
TEST **Baer
TEST **Baida
TEST **Banda
TEST **Bates
TEST **Bell
TEST **Bernstein
TEST **Bissot

LAST_NAME
---------------------------------------
TEST **Bloom
TEST **Bull
TEST **Cabrio
TEST **Cambrault
TEST **Cambrault
TEST **Chen
TEST **Chung
TEST **Colmenares

19 rows selected.

SQL> █
```

Comment

The protection mode of the database being maximum availability, there was a temporary difference between standby sites and the primary site, but once the connection is restored, the two have been automatically resynchronized. If the mode of protection was maximum protection, the primary instance would have been terminated upon completion of the COMMIT;

4 - Change the Delay of applying logs on the physical standby database to one hour.
-   Assign the value 130 to parameter log_archive_trace on the physical standby database.
-   On the primary database, with the user hr, change the last_name of employees to add Test SWITCH R * at the beginning of the name, commit the update and make a switch logfile
-   Make a permutation of roles between the primary database and physical standby database by SQL.
    What comments do you make?
-   Remake a permutation of roles between the two same databases, this time by Enterprise Manager.

Solution

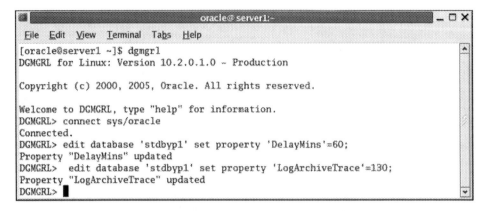

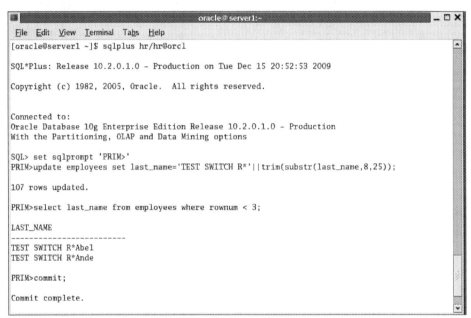

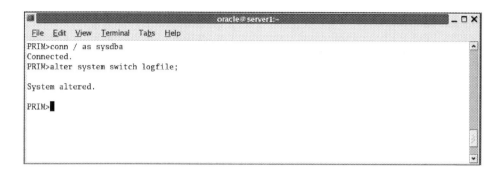

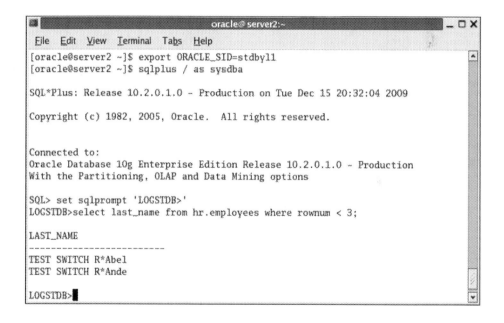

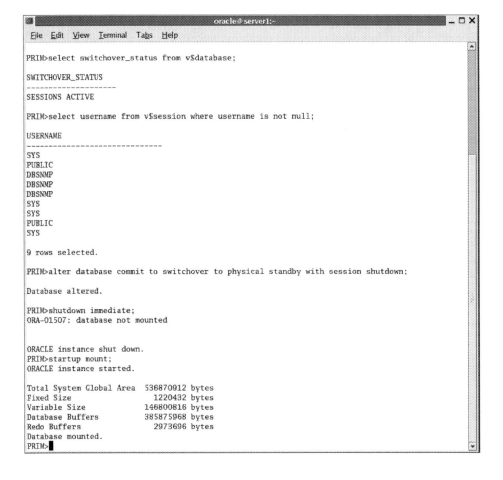

```
oracle@server1:~                                        _ □ X

File  Edit  View  Terminal  Tabs  Help

PRIM>select switchover_status from v$database;

SWITCHOVER_STATUS
---------------------
SESSIONS ACTIVE

PRIM>select username from v$session where username is not null;

USERNAME
------------------------------
SYS
PUBLIC
DBSNMP
DBSNMP
DBSNMP
SYS
SYS
PUBLIC
SYS

9 rows selected.

PRIM>alter database commit to switchover to physical standby with session shutdown;

Database altered.

PRIM>shutdown immediate;
ORA-01507: database not mounted


ORACLE instance shut down.
PRIM>startup mount;
ORACLE instance started.

Total System Global Area   536870912 bytes
Fixed Size                   1220432 bytes
Variable Size              146800816 bytes
Database Buffers           385875968 bytes
Redo Buffers                 2973696 bytes
Database mounted.
PRIM>
```

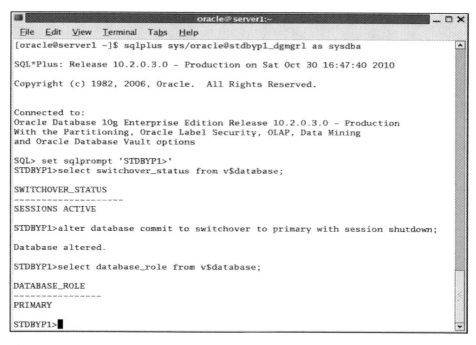

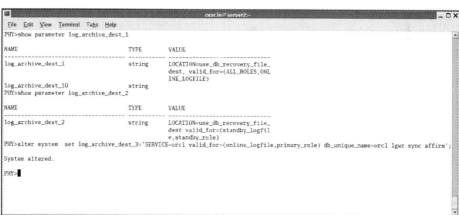

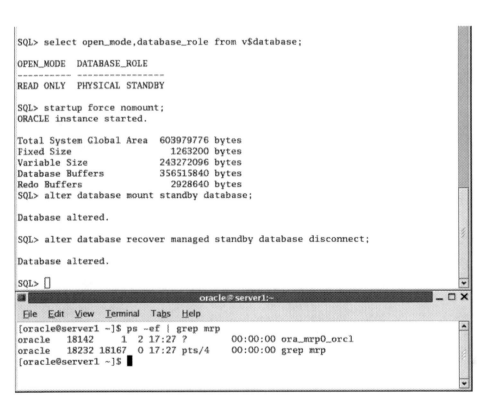

Switchover has been made by SQL, the status of Data Guard broker apperars in error, delete the standby databases by

```
DGMGRL> Remove database db_unique_name preserve
destinations;
```

and add them in the configuration.

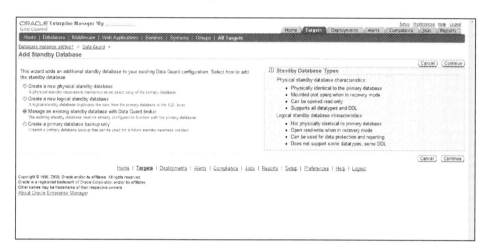

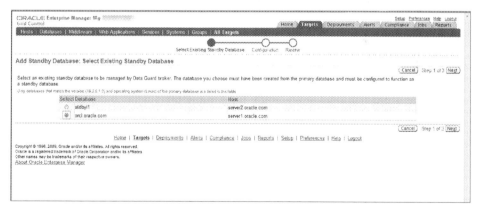

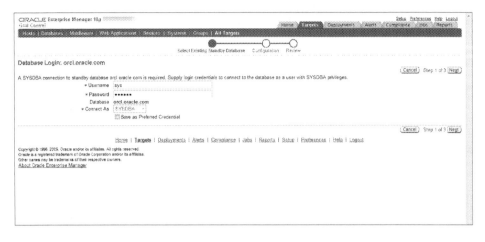

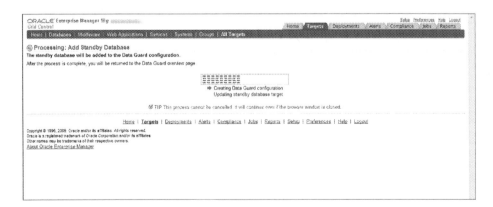

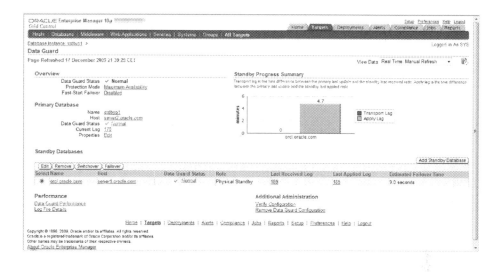

SWITCHOVER by Enterprise Manager

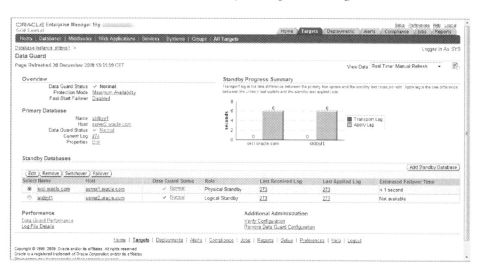

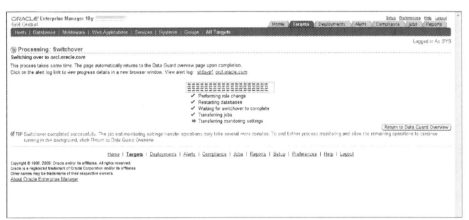

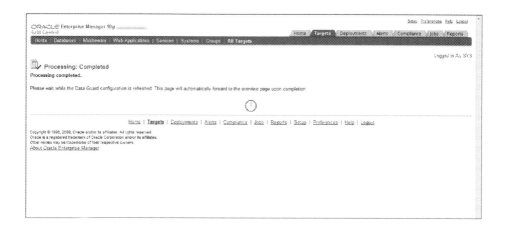

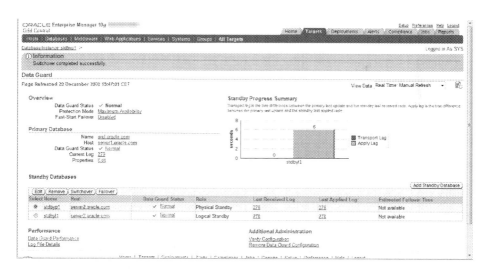

FAST START FAILOVER &
TRANSPARENT APPLICATION
FAILOVER

X-1 FAST START FAILOVER (FSFO)

FSFO is a feature of Data Guard since 10g R2 version which allows an automatic switch to a pre-designated standby database following a failure occurred in the primary database. This new feature eliminates the manual change of database after failure thus increasing the availability of your system.

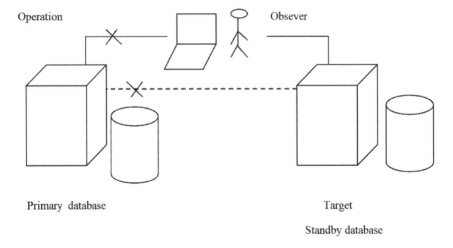

Primary database

Target

Standby database

The observer is a client-side component, which is conveniently installed on a computer, separated from the main database server and that of the standby database in order to avoid that one of those servers becomes a single point of failure.

A Fast-START FAILOVER is triggered in one of the following conditions:

- An instance failure occurs for a mono instance database, or all instances of a RAC database are down
- The primary base is stopped with abort option (shutdown abort)
- All data files from the primary database are offline
- A loss of connectivity occurs between the primary base and the observer or between the primary base and the target standby database FSFO.

Installation of the observer

The observer is a client-side component FSFO which may be available in 2 ways:

- When installing the Oracle software, select Administration. This option will install all the components including the Oracle client administration command line interface DGMGRL.
- After installing the "Oracle database server" that includes DGMGRL and Enterprise Manager.

Configuration of FSFO

We will describe the different configuration steps of FSFO. The commands used here are those of DGMGRL. You can also configure FSFO using Enterprise Manager Data Guard Broker.

1) Define the target standby database

```
DGMGRL> Edit database db_unique_primary set property
'FastStarFailoverTarget' = db_unique_standby;
```

In a configuration with a single standby database this step is not necessary.

2) Set the threshold of FSFO

The threshold is the delay in seconds after which the changeover takes place after finding the failure of the primary database. The default is 30 seconds.

DGMGRL> EDIT CONFIGURATION SET PROPERTY 'FASTSTARFAILOVERTHRESHOLD' = value;

☞ This value can be changed at any time.

3) Enable Fast start Failover;

DGMGRL>ENABLE FAST_START FAILOVER;

Prerequisites

- Existence of standby logfiles on the primary base and the target standby database;
- Transfer of logs with the option LGWR SYNC AFFIRM;
- Configuration Data Guard broker enabled ;
- Flashback database must be enabled on the primary database and the standby target;
- Type of protection of database being maximum Availability; (Note that this last condition requires the prior establishment of the first two).

4) Start the observer

DGMGRL>START OBSERVER [FILE =/path/file]

The file used by default is FSFO.dat, created in the current working directory

☞ Can be executed even if FSFO is disabled, but in this case the launching will never take place.
☞ It is a foreground process. The hand does not return after execution of this command, so it is advisable to run it in another terminal window.

☞ The Observer can be started in any host having interface DGMGRL regardless the Operating system type. But the version of the Observer must be greater or equal to the version of the Oracle Databases server to be observed.

E.G: You can launch the Observer in a post hosting Oracle Database server 11g on Windows to monitor oracle Databases server 10g running on LINUX on other servers; but you cannot launch the observer using DGMGRL 10g to monitor Oracle Databases server 11g

5) Check the configuration

DGMGRL> SHOW CONFIGURATION VERBOSE;

After enabling the FSFO, the followings actions are prohibited in the Data Guard:

- Change of the protection mode
- Change of the property of logXpt mode
- Failover or switchover with a standby database not target of FSFO
- Change of the standby database target of FSFO
- Disabling or deleting of the configuration DATA GUARD broker
- Disabling or removal of the standby database of FSFO

OTHER ACTIONS WITH FSFO

—Disabling FSFO

If you want to perform any of the above mentioned while FSFO is active, you must first disable it by

DGMGRL>DISABLE FAST_START FAILOVER [FORCE];

Note: This command does not stop the observer. The force option is to specify in the absence of connection between the primary database and target standby database, otherwise the command fails.

At the successful end of the execution of this command, Data Guard broker disables FSFO on the target database and then in the primary base. This change is recorded permanently then propagated to all standby databases of Data Guard configuration.

For an effective disabling, after loss of connectivity between the primary database and the target standby database, the command FSFO must have been executed either on the primary database or on a non target database with connectivity with the main base, or on the target database itself.

When running this command on a non target standby database with no connectivity with the primary base, the command is ignored on this one and FSFO becomes active on standby database once the connection reestablished.

—Stop of the observer

DGMGRL>STOP OBSERVER ;

This command does not affect the status of FSFO.
The command must be launched on the primary database or standby database that has a connectivity with the primary database.

☞ Note: The observer cannot be launched more than once for a data guard broker configuration. If you want to move the observer to another position, for example, consider to first stop on the old host before running on the new; otherwise you will get the error message ORA-16647.
"The observer could not start Because There Was Another observed Observing Already ..."

–Reinstate the primary database after a FSFO.

Reinstating of the original primary database after an FSFO transaction can be done automatically or not depending on certain conditions. Recovery is automatic when the following conditions are fulfilled:

- The original primary database has been repaired and started
- The observer can connect to the initial primary base and the latter has a connectivity with the new primary base
- If the Data Guard broker configuration has more than one standby database, no SWITCHOVER or FAILOVER was delivered prior to the restart of the original primary database.

If any of these conditions is not met, the automatic recovery attempt fails in this case, follow the manual reinstatement by

```
DGMGRL>Reinstate database db_unique_name ;
```

Dictionary information related to FSFO containing columns for FSFO

The V$database view contains columns for FSFO

FS _FAILOVER_ STATUS (FSFO status)

- DISABLED: FSFO disabled;
- BY STANDER: FSFO active, but the standby database where the view is accessed is not the target database;
- LOADING DICTIONARY: only for the logical standby database and means that the loading of the dictionary from the primary database is in progress;
- PRIMARY UNOBSERVED: indicates that the target standby database is synchronized with the primary database, but it (primary base) is not connected to the observer
- SYNCHRONIZED: the primary database and the target standby database are synchronized.
- UNSYNCHRONIZED: The primary base and the target standby are not synchronized (all redo log information generated

in the primary are not received on the target standby). In this case, the FSFO operation can't take place.

- STALLED: only on the primary database. If the latter is no longer connected to the target standby database, nor to the observer.
- SUSPENDED: only on the target database, if the latter or the primay base has been cleanly shut down (shutdown with option other than about)
- REINSTATE FAILED: reestablishment of the old primary database failed
- REINSTATE IN PROCESS: reestablishment of the old primary database is going on
- REINSTATE REQUIRED: reestablishment of the initial primary database required

- FS_FAILOVER_ CURRENT_TARGET : current target database
- FS_FAILOVER_THRESHOLD : threshold in seconds before initiating the operation FSFO
- FS_FAILOVER_OBSERVER_HOST: host on which the observer is executed
- FS_ FAILOVER_OBSERVER _PRESENT : indicates whether or not the observer is connected to the local database. Null if no observer.

X-2 TRANSPARENT APPLICATION FAILOVER (TAF)

We have seen how to enable the feature FSFO.
What happens with client connections when an automatic change of base occurs? If the connection configurations were made using the basic features of Oracle Net (by NetMGR, e.g.) they fail after release of FSFO because their tnsnames.ora entry (for example) always points on the primary database of origin if it is not changed manually.
In this case, customers do not enjoy full functionality of FSFO.
A maximum benefit is derived if the feature TRANSPARENT FAILOVER Application (TAF) is implemented

TAF is a feature of Oracle Net providing to clients Load balancing and Failover (contact with another network backup service in case of failure of the current service)

IMPLEMENTATION OF TAF

It is done by specifying the parameter FAILOVER_ MODE in the description section of tnsnames.ora file.

```
It can't be done using the graphic netmgr. You must
do it manually
```
(by a text editor).

```
Service-name =
(DESCRIPTION = (LOAD_BALANCE = ON) (FAILOVER_ON
(ADDRESS = ...)
(CONNECT_DATA = (SERVICE_NAME = ....)
(FAILOVER_MODE = (TYPE =) (METHOD =)
(BACKUP =) (= RETR) (DELAY =))))
FAILOVER_MODE contains five sub parameters:
TYPE, METHOD, BACUP, RETRIES, AND DELAY
```

TYPE: Specifies the type of failover that can be:

> SESSION Activates failover for the session if a user connection is lost, a new one is created for that user on the network server specified in the backup. This type does not recover the instances select going on during the failure.
> SELECT Works like the previous type but with recovery of the select statement in progress during the failure statement while the active transactions are being canceled.
> NONE no failover, default type

METHOD: Determines how fast failover of the primary node to the backup node is made: takes two possible values;

BASIC connection to the standby network service is made in case of failure on the primary node (NO CONNECTION IS PERDETERMINED)

PRECONNECT the connection to the standby service is established (without waiting for the failure towards the primary service). This allows fast switching but can cause an overload of connection on the standby service

BACKUP: Designates the name of the backup service network, present in the file tnsnames. ora

RETRIES: Specifies the number of login attempts after a failure, if delay is specified, the default value of retries is 5

DELAY: Time in seconds to wait before retries. If Retries is specified, delay's default is 1 second.

☞ These two values must be sized so that their product is greater than the threshold of the FSFO triggering.

Example: TAF with a Pre-Establishing Connection

A backup connection can be pre-established. The initial and backup connections must be explicitly specified.

```
orcl_dgmgrl=

(DESCRIPTION=
  (ADDRESS=
      (PROTOCOL=tcp)
      (HOST=server1)
      (PORT=1521))
  (CONNECT_DATA=
      (SERVICE_NAME=orcl_DGMGRL.oracle.com)
      (INSTANCE_NAME=orcl)
      (FAILOVER_MODE=
        (BACKUP=stdbyp1_dgmgrl)
        (TYPE=select)
        (METHOD=preconnect))))
stdbyp1_dgmgrl=
(DESCRIPTION=
  (ADDRESS=
      (PROTOCOL=tcp)
      (HOST=server2)
      (PORT=1522))
  (CONNECT_DATA=
      (SERVICE_NAME=stdbyp1_DGMGRL.oracle.com)
      (INSTANCE_NAME=stdbyp1)
      (FAILOVER_MODE=
        (BACKUP=orcl_dgmgrl)
        (TYPE=select)
  (METHOD=preconnect))))
```

MONITORING TAF

You can monitor the operation of TAF consulting the columns FAILED_OVER, FAILOVER_TYPE and FAILOVER_METHOD of the V$SESSION view. FAILED_OVER contains YES if Failover is enabled and NO otherwise.

EXERCISE

1) Install the observer, designate as the target database stdbyp1 and enable FSFO

The configuration of FSFO (designation of the of observer) is made by Enterprise Manager on a single page.

If a condition of activation FSFO is not met, it will be flagged.
We can also do it by DGMGRL.

```
DGMGRL>connect sys/oracle@primorcl
DGMGRL> Edit database orcl set property
'FastStartFailoverTarget'='stdbyp1';
DGMGRL>Edit configuration set property
'FastStartFailoverthreshold'= 45
DGMGRL>Enable Fast_Start Failover;
DGMGRL>Start Observer file = C:\FSFO\file.dat
```

2) Configure TAF in your tnsnames.ora file with
Backup service stdbyp1
mode PRECONNECT
Type = SELECT
Retries = 5 delay = 15 s

The physical standby database being in MOUNT mode, the preconnect can't be established on this base, we use the basic method, on the other hand, the method preconnect can be established on the primary database.

Tnsnames.ora Network Configuration File: G: \ oracle \ product \ 10.2.0 \ db_1 \ NETWORK \ ADMIN \ tnsnames.ora
Generated by Oracle configuration tools.

= LISTENER_ORCL2
(ADDRESS = (PROTOCOL =TCP) (HOST =TRAIN.ORACLE. COM) (PORT = 1522))

ORCLdg =
(DESCRIPTION =
  (ADDRESS_LIST =
    (ADDRESS = (PROTOCOL = TCP) (HOST = 192.168.0.1) (PORT = 1521)))
      (CONNECT_DATA = (SERVICE_NAME = orcl.oracle. com)))
ORCLTAF =
(DESCRIPTION =(ADDRESS = (PROTOCOL = TCP) (HOST = server1)
  (PORT = 1521))
    (CONNECT_DATA = (SERVICE_NAME = orcl_dgmgrl. oracle.com)
    (Instance_name = orcl)
    (FAILOVER_MODE =
      (BACKUP = stdbyp1_dgmgrl)
      (TYPE = select)
      (METHOD = basic)
      (RETR = 5) (DELAY = 15))))
standbyp1_dgmgrl =
(DESCRIPTION =
  (ADDRESS = (PROTOCOL = TCP) (HOST = server2) (PORT = 1522))
    (CONNECT_DATA= (SERVICE_NAME = stdbyp1_ DGMGRL.oracle.com)

```
    (Instance_name = stdbyp1)
    (FAILOVER_MODE=
      (BACKUP = ORCLTAF)
      (TYPE = select)
      (METHOD = preconnect)
      (RETR 5) (DELAY = 15))))
ORCL2 =
(DESCRIPTION =
  (ADDRESS_LIST=
    (ADDRESS  =  (PROTOCOL  =  TCP)  (HOST  =  TRAIN.
    ORACLE.COM)
(PORT = 1522))
    (CONNECT_DATA =(SERVER = DEDICATED)
    (SERVICE_NAME = orcl2)
ORCL =
(DESCRIPTION =
  (ADDRESS_LIST =
    (ADDRESS  =  (PROTOCOL  =  TCP)  (HOST  =  TRAIN.
    ORACLE.COM)
(PORT = 1522)) )
    (CONNECT_DATA = (SERVER = DEDICATED)
    (SERVICE_NAME = orcl)))
    EXTPROC_CONNECTION_DATA =
    (DESCRIPTION =
      (ADDRESS_LIST =
        (ADDRESS = (PROTOCOL = IPC) (KEY = EXTPROC1)))
        (CONNECT_DATA =
        (SID = PLSExtProc)
        (PRESENTATION = RO)))
```

3) Open a session with hr. Display the first 4 names of employees.
   Check the columns for TAF and FSFO in the primary and in
   the logical standby database.

```
SQL*Plus: Release 10.2.0.2.0—Production on Sun Dec
20 21:02:13 2009
Copyright  (c)  1982,  2005,  Oracle.  All  Rights
Reserved.
```

```
SQL> conn hr/hr@ORCLTAF
Connected.
SQL>set sqlprompt 'HRTAF>';
HRTAF> select last_name from employees where rownum
< 5;


LAST_NAME
--------------------------
TEST SWITCH R*Abel
TEST SWITCH R*Ande
TEST SWITCH R*Atkinson
TEST SWITCH R*Austin
HRTAF>
```

We check the FSFO status in the logical standby and check it again in
the primary database opening two other sessions SQL.

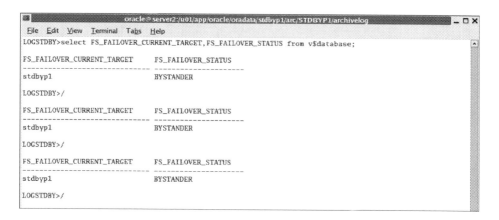

We see that on the logical standby database, which is not the target
database of FSFO, the column FS_FAILOVER_STATUS contains 'BY
STANDER'

```
SQL> select fs_failover_current_target,fs_failover_
status from v$database;
```

```
FS_FAILOVER_CURRENT_TARGET    FS_FAILOVER_STATUS
---------------------------   -------------------
stdbyp1                       SYNCHRONIZED
```

While in the physical standby database target of FSFO, this status is "SYNCHRONIZED"

We check the failover status in orcl instance

```
SQL>set SQLPROMPT 'ORCL_SYSTEM>'

ORCL_SYSTEM>  select   failed_over,failover_method,
failover_type from v$session where username='HR';

FAI FAILOVER_M    FAILOVER_TYPE
--------------    --------------
NO  BASIC         SELECT
```

4) **Shut down abort the primary instance orcl, wait 45" and rechecks the views above, return to the session HR and refresh the query. What do you observe?**

```
oracle@server1:~
File  Edit  View  Terminal  Tabs  Help
SQL> select * from v$instance;

INSTANCE_NUMBER INSTANCE_NAME
--------------- -----------------
HOST_NAME
--------------------------------------------------------------
VERSION         STARTUP_T STATUS    PAR   THREAD# ARCHIVE LOG_SWITCH_WAIT
--------------- --------- --------- ---   ------- ------- ---------------
LOGINS    SHU DATABASE_STATUS   INSTANCE_ROLE      ACTIVE_ST BLO
--------- --- ----------------- ------------------ --------- ---
              1 orcl
server1.oracle.com
10.2.0.1.0        20-DEC-09 OPEN      NO          1 STARTED
ALLOWED   NO  ACTIVE            PRIMARY_INSTANCE   NORMAL    NO

SQL> shutdown abort;
ORACLE instance shut down.
```

```
SQL> conn sys/oracle@stdbyp1_dgmgrl as sysdba
Connected.
```

```
SQL> select fs_failover_current_target, fs_failover_
status from v$database;


FS_FAILOVER_CURRENT_TARGET   FS_FAILOVER_STATUS
--------------------------   ------------------
orcl                         REINSTATE REQUIRED
SQL>set SQLPROMPT 'STDBYP1>'
STDBYP1>
```

Returning to the the session ORCL_SYSTEM, we refresh the query

```
ORCL_SYSTEM> /

select failed_over, failover_method, failover_type
from v$session where username='HR'

*ERROR at line 1:

ORA-03113: end-of-file on communication channel
```

The query fails, normal because the instance orcl is down and this connection does not use TAF

```
ORCL_SYSTEM > spool off

SQL*Plus: Release 10.2.0.2.0—Production on Sun Dec
20 21:02:13 2009

Copyright (c) 1982, 2005, Oracle. All Rights Reserved.
```

After 45" the target database stdbyp1 became the primary base and the connection of hr is directed to this latter. We return to the session HR where the instruction was running and refresh the query :

```
HRTAF> /
LAST_NAME
-------------------------
TEST SWITCH * R Abel
TEST SWITCH R * Ande
TEST SWITCH * R Atkinson
TEST SWITCH R * Austin
SQL>
```

After a few seconds (waiting for the FSFO and the delay of the TAF process)

The result is displayed. As the select method has been chosen, the results of the query are not lost.

5) Restart the instance orcl

```
SQL> startup;
ORACLE instance started.

Total System Global Area  536870912 bytes
Fixed Size                  1220432 bytes
Variable Size             163578032 bytes
Database Buffers          369098752 bytes
Redo Buffers                2973696 bytes
Database mounted.
ORA-16649: database will open after Data Guard broker has evaluated Fast-Start
Failover status


SQL> exit
ERROR:
ORA-03135: connection lost contact


Disconnected from Oracle Database 10g Enterprise Edition Release 10.2.0.1.0 - Production
With the Partitioning, OLAP and Data Mining options (with complications)
[oracle@server1 ~]$ oerr ora 16649
16649, 0000, "database will open after Data Guard broker has evaluated Fast-Start Failover status"
// *Cause:  The database is being opened while Fast-Start failover is enabled.
//          The message indicates that the Data Guard broker will first
//          determine if conditions are suitable for opening; that is, a
//          Fast-Start failover did not occur while the database was
//          unavailable.
// *Action: No action is normally required. The Data Guard broker will continue
//          opening the database after determining a Fast-Start failover did
//          not occur. If there is a chance that a Fast-Start Failover did
//          occur, the database will remain in the mounted state and will not
//          open. In this case, check the target standby to see if a role
//          transition took place.
```

After restarting, the instance orcl is reinstated automatically, during this automatic reinstatement, you may see errors.

Ora 16449:" database will open after a Data Guard broker Has Evaluated FSFO status" and Ora 16817 "unsynchronized FSFO config".

These "errors" indicate that the automatic reinstatement is going on.

You can see the progress of this reinstatement:

1) In SQL session

```
STDBYP1> /

FS_FAILOVER_CURRENT_TARGET     FS_FAILOVER_STATUS
---------------------------    --------------------
orcl                           REINSTATE REQUIRED

STDBYP1> /

FS_FAILOVER_CURRENT_TARGET     FS_FAILOVER_STATUS
---------------------------    --------------------
orcl                           REINSTATE IN PROGRESS
STDBYP1> /

FS_FAILOVER_CURRENT_TARGET     FS_FAILOVER_STATUS
---------------------------    --------------------
orcl                           SYNCHRONIZED
```

The status of fast_start FAILOVER progresses from "REINSTATE REQUIRED" TO "SYNCHRONIZED"

2) In the DGMGRL session where the observer has been started

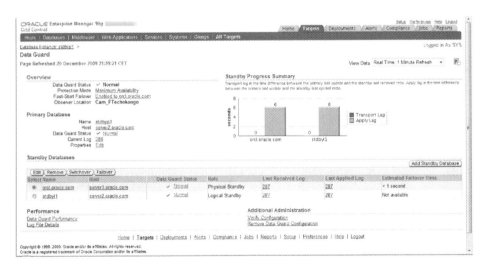

3) In Enterprise Manager

Activate the auto display data in Enterprise Manager and you will see at the end of the reinstatement is well done.

5 - Restore the original roles of primary bases and logical standby databases

SWITCHOVER is impossible with database not target of FSFO, while FSFO is database is not synchronized with the PRIMARY, the switchover is also impossible. We proceed by abnormally stopping standbyp1 and restart after 2 minutes to allow auto reinstatement.

## CHAPTER 11

OTHER ACCOUNTS RELATED TO DATA GUARD

FLASHBACK DATABASE AND DATA GUARD

Attention must be paid when flashback database is performed on a database in a Data Guard configuration:

a) When the flashback database command returns a logical standby database at a time prior to an operation of switchover roles, the database returns to its role at that moment.

b) On the other hand, if the flashback database operation is performed on a physical standby database, the database preserves the role it had at the time of the switchover.

c) Flashback database can be used to cancel the activation of a physical standby database.

Up to 10g R2, the physical standby database could be only opened in read-only, in this mode, the production of certain reports is impossible if DML or DDL operations are necessary. To solve this, you can temporarily convert the physical standby database to the primary database by activating it, produce reports on this database and then return to it original by a flashback database command (We will develop it in the next pages).

Should a flashback database be done on the standby database after having been made on the primary base?

A flashback on the standby database is needed only if it is ahead on the primary database. For this, we compare the CURRENT _SCN of the standby database with the RESETLOGS _CHANGE $\neq$ column of the V$database view in the primary database.

- On the primary database, the column Resetlogs_change # gives us the SCN after the flashback operation.
- On the standby database, the column CURRENT_SCN of the V$database view gives us the present SCN

A comparison is made between the two values
If CURRENT_SCN is greater than RESETLOGS_CHANGE #—2
Then Flashback to RESETLOGS_ CHANGE#.
If not, no flashback is required, the standby is back from the primary database, apply of logs on this standby will bring it to the same level as the primary database.

Remark The SCN of a database is still increasing even after a reincarnation of it. For this reason, you cannot use the field CURRENT_SCN but rather RESETLOGS_CHANGE# which records the SCN after a flashback database. You can get the SCN after a flashback database by consulting the field CURRENT_ SCN but **database opened in read only** mode before the opening with the RESETLOGS option.

TEMPORARY ACTIVATION OF A PHYSICAL STANDBY DATABASE

We saw previously that in some cases, we should activate temporarily a physical standby database for reportings or testing purposes.
To do it, proceed as follows :

Step 1—In the Standby database

A) Set up a flash recovery area as seen previously
B) Cancel Redo Apply and create a guaranteed restore point.
```
SQL> ALTER DATABASE RECOVER MANAGED STANDBY DATABASE
CANCEL;
SQL> CREATE RESTORE POINT Standby_flashback_test
GUARANTEE FLASHBACK  DATABASE;
```

Step 2—In the Primary Database

A) On the primary database, switch logs so the SCN of the restore point will be archived on the physical standby database. When using standby redo logfiles, this step is essential to ensure the database can be properly flashed back to the restore point.

```
SQL> ALTER SYSTEM ARCHIVE LOG CURRENT;
```

B) Defer log archive destinations pointing to the standby that will be activated.

```
SQL> ALTER SYSTEM SET LOG_ARCHIVE_DEST_
STATE_2=DEFER;
```

Step 3—In the Standby database

A) Activate the physical standby database:

```
SQL> ALTER DATABASE ACTIVATE STANDBY DATABASE;
```

Once it's done, you can check that the control file status has been changed from Standby to Current and database role to Primary

```
SQL> select CONTROLFILE_TYPE, DATABASE _ROLE from
v$database;

CONTROL DATABASE_ROLE
----------------------
CURRENT PRIMARY
```

B) Then open the database.

```
SQL> ALTER DATABASE OPEN;
```

Step 4—In the old Standby database

Once the standby database has been activated, you can run reporting tools or perform other testing and activities for as long as desired, independent of the initial primary database.

Step 5—In the old standby database

A) Revert the active standby database back to Physical standby database

A1. Mount the database.
A2. Flashback the database to restore point.

```
SQL> SHUTDOWN IMMEDIATE;
SQL> STARTUP MOUNT;
SQL> FLASHBACK DATABASE TO RESTORE POINT Standby_
flashback_test ;
```

You can confirm the same by checking the control file status. It will be now backup controlfile, but the database role is still primary.

```
SQL> select controlfile_type,database_role from
v$database;


CONTROL DATABASE _ROLE
----------------------
BACKUP PRIMARY
```

At this step, the database has not yet become a standby database, you must convert it.

B) Convert to Standby database and put the standby database in managed recovery mode

```
SQL> ALTER DATABASE CONVERT TO PHYSICAL STANDBY;
SQL> STARTUP MOUNT FORCE;
SQL> ALTER DATABASE RECOVER MANAGED STANDBY DATABASE
DISCONNECT;
```

You can check the new status of the database by:

SQL> select controlfile_type, database_role from v$database;

```
CONTROL DATABASE_ROLE
-----------------------
STANDBY PAYSICAL STANDBY
```

Let archive gap resolution fetch all missing archived redo log files.

Step 6—In the Primary database

A) Re-enable archiving to the physical standby database:

```
SQL> ALTER SYSTEM ARCHIVE LOG CURRENT;
SQL> ALTER SYSTEM SET LOG_ARCHIVE_DEST_STATE_2=ENABLE;
```

Step 7—In the Standby database

Drop the restore point

```
SQL> DROP RESTORE POINT Standby_flashback_testing ;
```

Caution:

While the database is activated, it is not receiving redo data from the primary database and cannot provide disaster protection. It is recommended that you have at least two physical standby databases participating in the configuration so that the primary database remains protected against data loss.

MANAGING A SNAPSHOT STANDBY DATABASE

< Version 11g only >

A snapshot standby database, present only in 11g version is a type of physical standby database that a can be opened in READ-WRITE mode. It is created by converting a physical standby database. Redo logfiles received are not applied, they will be applied when the database will be reverted back to a normal standby database. The apply process will start after discarding automatically all updates made locally by the users so the contents of both primary and standby databases will be equivalent.

This kind of standby database thus offers us the following benefits:

- Tests can be conducted on it
- The protection against loss is still ensured
- Contrary to a logical standby database where updates are also permitted, there will not be divergence between the primary and the physical standby after applying the redo data received.

Converting a physical standby database into a snapshot standby database.

To convert into a snapshot standby database, proceed as follows:

1) Ensure that the flash recovery area is set in the standby database
2) Stop all the instances except one if in RAC mode
3) Set the instance in MOUNT mode
4) Stop the REDO Apply if it is running.
5) Perform the conversion by the SQL command.

```
SOL>AlTER DATABASE CONVERT TO SNAPSHOT STANDBY;
```

Can also be done with DGMGRL command:

```
DGMGRL>CONVERT DATABASE <db_unique_name> TO SNAPSHOT
STANDBY;
```

Reverting back to a physical standby database

To convert a snapshot standby database into a physical standby database, proceed as follows:

1) Shutdown all the instances except one if in RAC mode
2) Ensure that the database is in MOUNT MODE
3) Perform the conversion issuing :

```
SOL> ALTER DATABASE CONVERT TO PHYSICAL STANDBY;
                      OR
DGMGRL > CONVERT DATABASE db_unique_name TO PHYSICAL
STANDBY;
```

At the successful end of this command, the instance will be shutdown and needs to be restarted manually

4) Restart the REDO APPLY

Accounts related to a snapshot standby database

- A snapshot standby database can't be used for a FAILOVER or a SWITCHOVER (It must be first converted into a normal physical standby database)
- To enable MAXIMUM protection mode, you must have in your data Guard configuration another standby database.
- As flashback database is used (automatically) to revert a snapshot standby database back to a physical standby database, operations preventing the execution of a flashback database as we saw in section "flashback database" on page 102 will make fail the revert operation.

DATA GUARD & BACKUPS

CASES OF THE USE OF A PHYSICAL STANDBY DATABASE

The primary database and the physical standby database must use the same recovery catalog, the two bases having physically identical database blocks, their backups (of data and archive logs) are interchangeable, provided they have been performed by RMAN in catalog mode.

The backup control files are never interchangeable. Once the primary database registered in the catalog an attempt to register the physical standby database generates an error because both have the same identifier database (DBID)

Presentation of the technical environment used for the workshops and examples in this book.

- Server hosting OMS (Oracle Management Service) and the repository OMR named server2
- Server hosting the database production and OMA(Oracle Management Agent) named server1

A) INSTALLATION OF ENTERPRISE MANAGER GRID CONTROL

The latest version of Enterprise Manager Grid Control (10.2.0.5) at the time of writing this book is used for tutorials and examples in this book. We describe below the installation procedure.

A-1 INSTALLATION OF OMS ON THE HOST SERVER2

After checking the prerequisites needed to install Grid control, start the installation:

$ cd <directory_install>

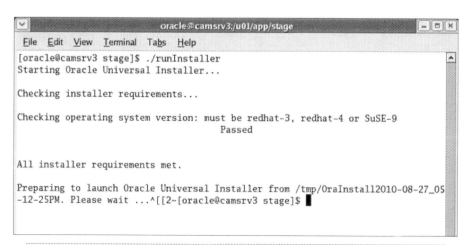

```
oracle@camsrv3:/u01/app/stage
File  Edit  View  Terminal  Tabs  Help
[oracle@camsrv3 stage]$ ./runInstaller
Starting Oracle Universal Installer...

Checking installer requirements...

Checking operating system version: must be redhat-3, redhat-4 or SuSE-9
                              Passed


All installer requirements met.

Preparing to launch Oracle Universal Installer from /tmp/OraInstall2010-08-27_05
-12-25PM. Please wait ...^[[2~[oracle@camsrv3 stage]$ █
```

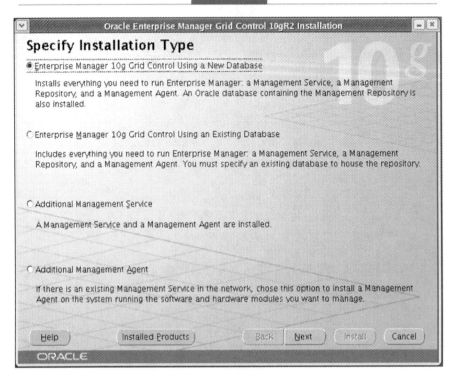

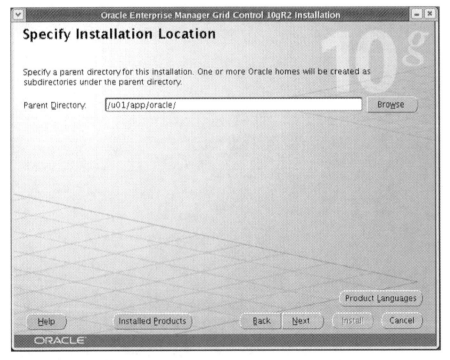

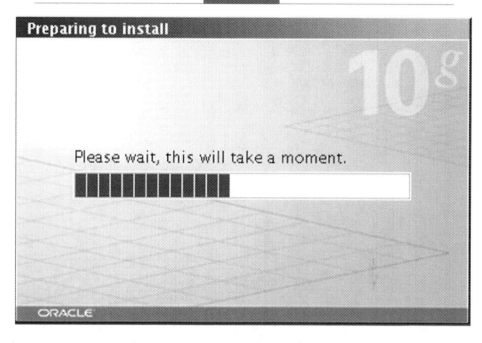

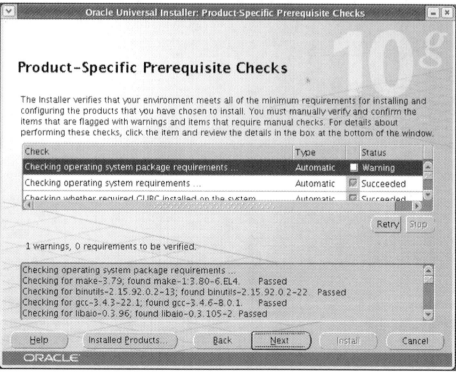

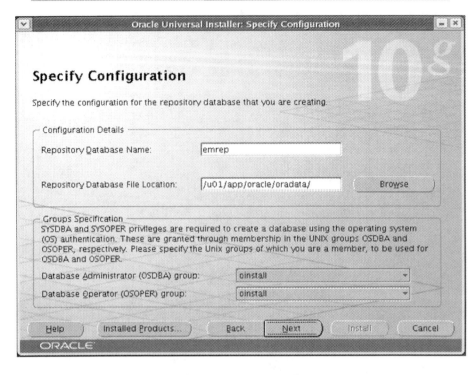

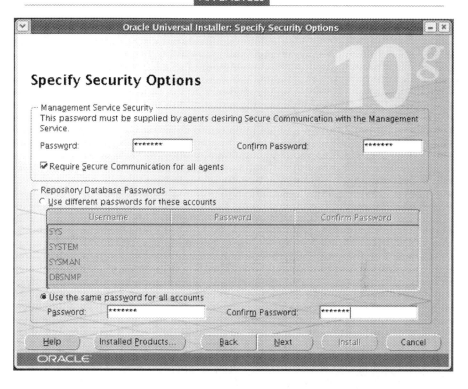

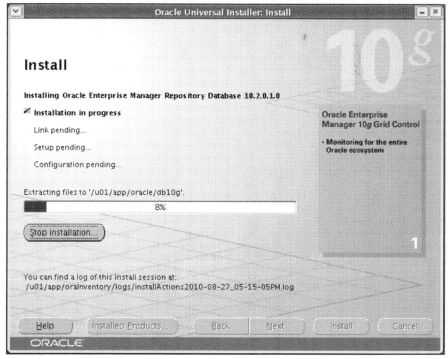

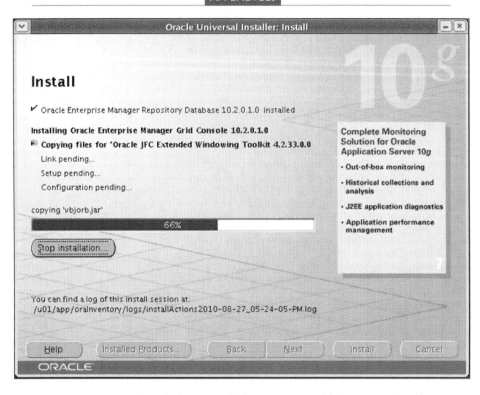

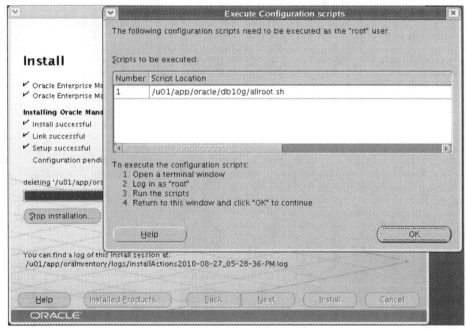

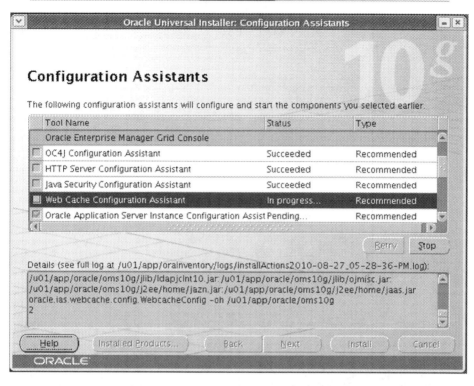

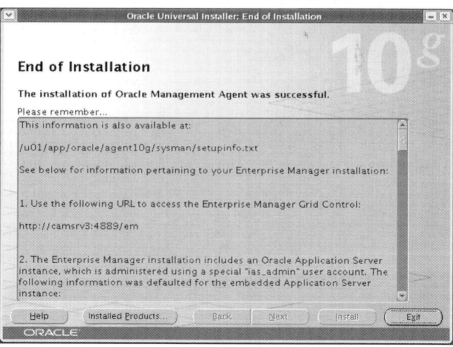

The Grid Control Console is accessible via the link http://server2:4889/em After installation, perform the upgrade to version 10.2.0.5. For the Linux version, see
http://www. oracle.com / technetword /otn/ grid-control /downloads /linux-soft099441. html and follow the instructions in the readme file to process the upgrade.

Caution:
For version 10.2.0.5 on Linux, agent files sources are not present in $OMS_ HOME/sysman/agent_download, download them from oracle site (http:// www.oracle.com/technology/sofware/products/oem/htdocs/agent soft. html) then follow the instructions provided in the file instructions.txt

A-2 INSTALLATION OF THE AGENT ON THE HOST SERVER1

There are several ways to install the agent OMS on the server some of which are:

- Interactive installation using OUI
- Installing the agent by the pull method using the script agent download
- Installation of the agent by the method agent deploy (push)

The method agent deploy also known as PUSH methods allows from the OMS server to deploy on client machines. It is recommended when there is a massive deployment to do.

Installation of the agent by the method Deploy agent (push)

- On root, create a symbolic link, the pgm sudo is in /usr/ bin and not in /usr/local/ bin.
  # ln-s /usr/ bin/sudo /usr/local/ bin/sudo
  on all servers to deploy.
- Sudo privilege must be assigned to the oracle user running the command
  Visudo on all servers to deploy as follows:
  #visudo

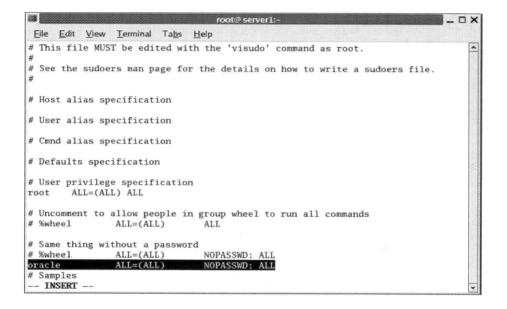

- In the OMS host (server2) with user oracle, run the script sshUserSetup.sh to prepare the deployment witch will be done using enterprise manager.

```
$ cd $OMS_HOME/sysman/prov/resources/scripts
```

```
oracle@server2:/u01/app/oracle/oms10g/oms10g/sysman/prov/resources/scripts  _ □ ×

Fichier  Édition  Affichage  Terminal  Onglets  Aide

[oracle@server2 scripts]$ ./sshUserSetup.sh -hosts server1 -user oracle
The output of this script is also logged into /tmp/sshUserSetup_2009-09-30-13-46
-27.log
Hosts are server1
user is oracle
Platform:~ Linux
Checking if the remote hosts are reachable
PING server1.oracle.com (192.168.0.1) 56(84) bytes of data.
64 bytes from server1.oracle.com (192.168.0.1): icmp_seq=0 ttl=64 time=2.53 ms
64 bytes from server1.oracle.com (192.168.0.1): icmp_seq=1 ttl=64 time=0.112 ms
64 bytes from server1.oracle.com (192.168.0.1): icmp_seq=2 ttl=64 time=0.112 ms
64 bytes from server1.oracle.com (192.168.0.1): icmp_seq=3 ttl=64 time=0.115 ms
64 bytes from server1.oracle.com (192.168.0.1): icmp_seq=4 ttl=64 time=0.119 ms

--- server1.oracle.com ping statistics ---
5 packets transmitted, 5 received, 0% packet loss, time 4000ms
rtt min/avg/max/mdev = 0.112/0.598/2.536/0.969 ms, pipe 2
Remote host reachability check succeeded.
The following hosts are reachable: server1.
The following hosts are not reachable: .
All hosts are reachable. Proceeding further...
firsthost server1
numhosts 1
The script will setup SSH connectivity from the host server2.oracle.com to all
```

- Proceed to the deployment using enterprise manager Grid Control

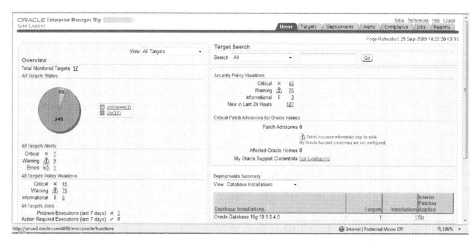

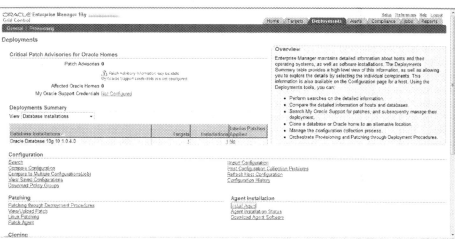

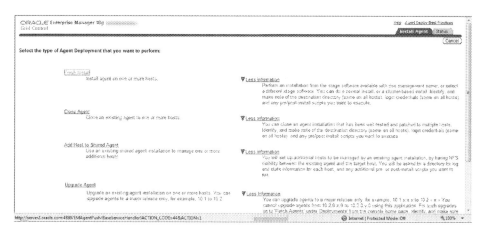

Specify Time Tone, otherwise an error will occur in the verification phase of the prerequisites with the message :

"Direct connection to OCM Server is not available."

This specification can be done in two ways:

- Either by typing-z <time zone> in the Additional Parameters field, eg
  - z Europe / Paris.

- Or by assigning a value to the environment variable TZ in the. bash_profile file of the user.

  $export TZ =Europe / Paris

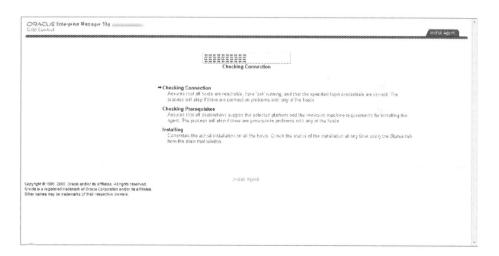

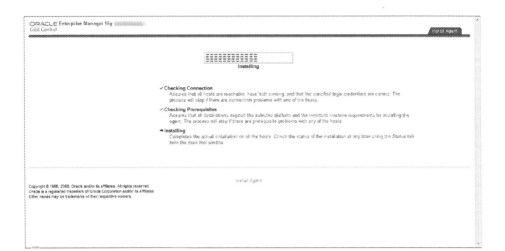

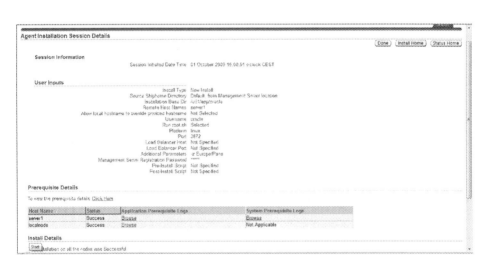

Remark:

After the installation and upgrade of OMS and OMA, the two start automatically when the server and the posts start:

- On the server hosting and OMS and OMA, the instance of the database is launched automatically, the database opened and all processes necessary for the management of OMS are launched.
- On the posts where are installed OMA agents, they are automatically started at the start of these posts

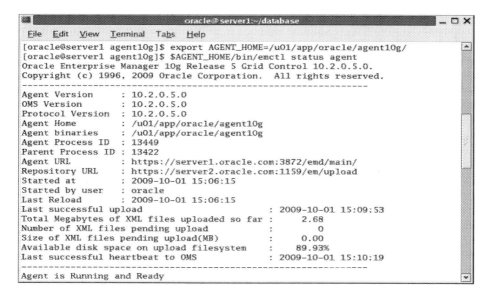

B) CREATION OF THE orcl DATABASE

An orcl database is used for the tutorials of this book. You can create it using the graphical wizard DBCA (Database Configuration Assistant)
$ dbca

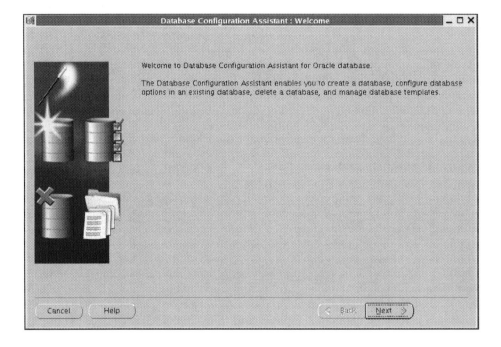

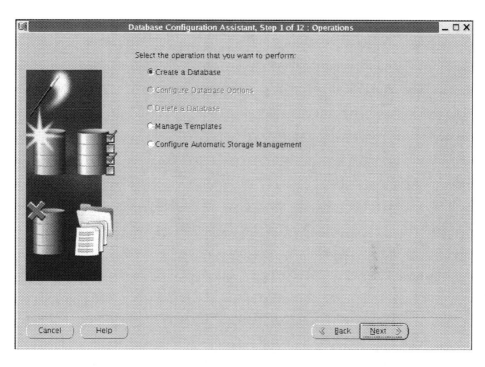

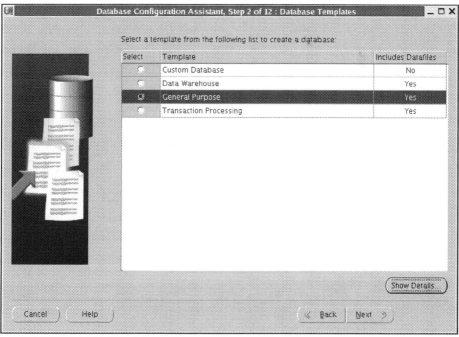

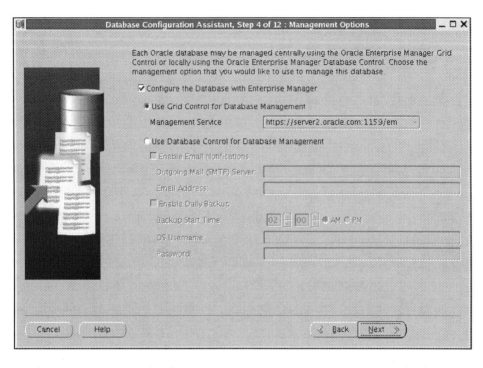

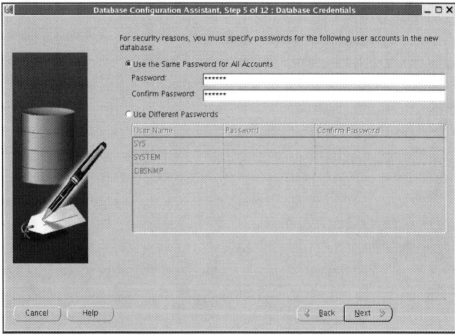

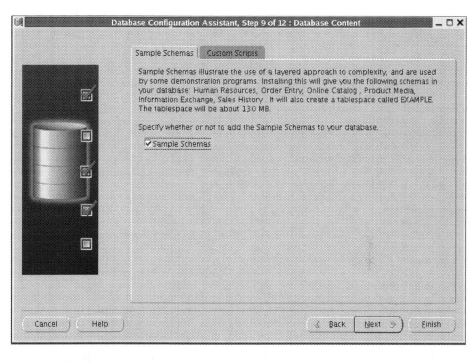

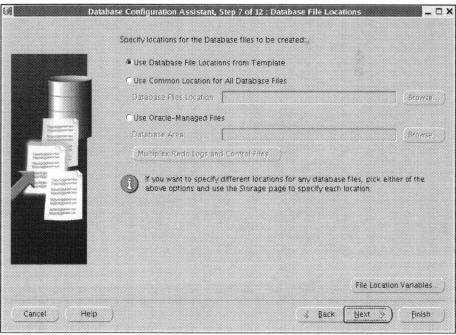

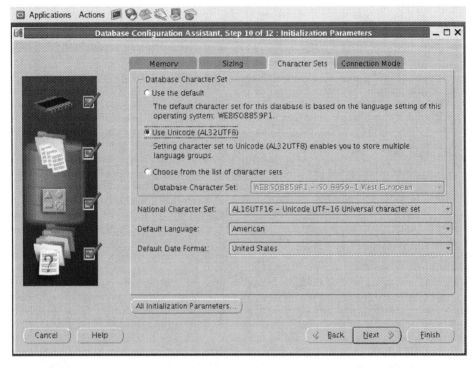

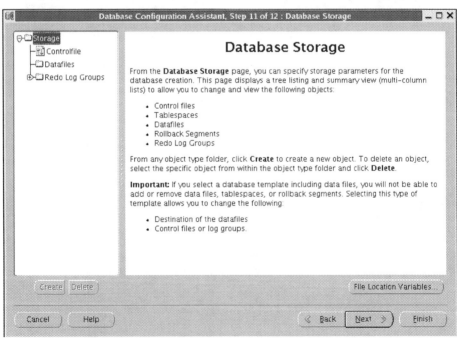

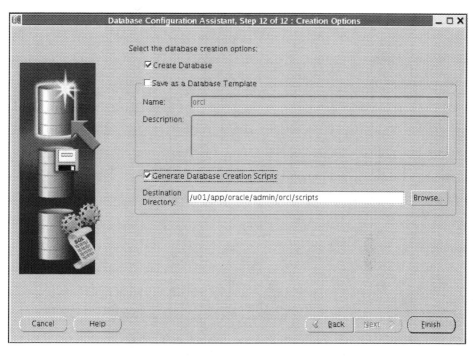

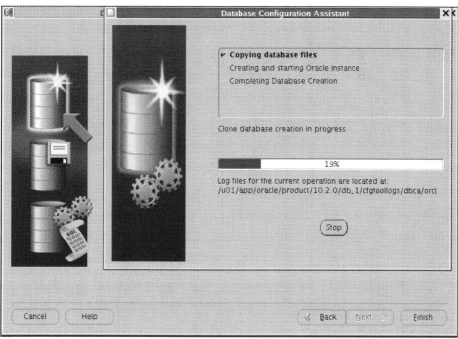

INDEX

ORACLE

PROTECT YOUR DATA
Floribert TCHOKONGOUE

Telecom Paris Engineer and Oracle Certified Master, **Floribert TCHOKONGOUE** is a senior consultant technology at CATALYST BUSINESS SOLUTIONS, Oracle platinum partner. He has 27 years experience in the IT industry with 15 years in Oracle Server technologies.

During all these years, he teaches both the standard as advanced database trainings in Oracle University classes covering:

- Real Application Clusters (RAC), Performance & Tuning
- Advanced Backups, Application Server
- Grid Control, Database Security
- Data Guard, Oracle Streams, . . .

Building on his long experience of administering databases (from version 7 to 11g), and trainings delivered, he designed this book as a course. Each concept developed begins with a theoretical description followed by examples and workshops where frequent encountered errors are highlighted. This teaching approach can meet the expectations of the beginners and those (students, engineers, project managers) who have a first experience in the administration of a version of Oracle.

The software (ORACLE RDBMS and Linux) needed for the practices developed in this book are downloadable free on the sites:

- ✓ http://www.oracle.com/technetwork/database/enterprise-edition/downloads/index.html (For a training purpose only)
- ✓ https://edelivery.oracle.com/linux